PARSONAGES

Kate Tiller

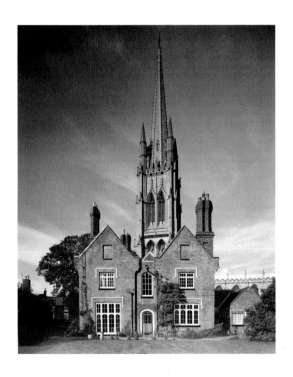

Published in Great Britain in 2016 by Shire Publications Ltd (part of Bloomsbury Publishing Plc), PO Box 883, Oxford, OX1 9PL, UK.
PO Box 3985, New York, NY 10185-3985, USA.

E-mail: shire@shirebooks.co.uk   www.shirebooks.co.uk

A CIP catalogue record for this book is available from the British Library.

Shire Library no. 786.   ISBN-13: 978 1 78442 137 3
PDF e-book ISBN: 978 1 78442 133 5
Epub ISBN: 978 1 78442 132 8

Typeset in Garamond Pro and Gill Sans.

Printed in China through World Print Ltd.

16 17 18 19 20   10 9 8 7 6 5 4 3 2 1

ACKNOWLEDGEMENTS
Kate Tiller would like to thank the following for their help and advice: James and Tina Bond, John Chandler, David Dymond, Evelyn Lord, Benjamin Richards, Adrienne Rosen, Marian Shaw, Simon Townley, Geoffrey Tyack, and especially Liam Tiller, who has developed an unexpected interest in parsonages and contributed invaluable expertise and support in preparing illustrations.

COVER IMAGE
Cover design and photography by Peter Ashley. Front cover: Old Rectory, Hallaton, Leicestershire (c. 1840). Back cover: Detail from a Player's cigarette card: Doctor Portman, rector in Pendennis by William Makepeace Thackeray. (Collection of Peter Ashley)

TITLE PAGE IMAGE
The vicarage at Louth, Lincolnshire, designed in 1832. (Martin Charles/RIBA Library Photographs Collection) (See page 48)

CONTENTS PAGE IMAGE
An example of the increasingly gentlemanly style of eighteenth-century parsonages, at Farnborough, Berkshire (1749), which was later home to John Betjeman (see page 45).

Shire Publications is supporting the Woodland Trust, the UK's leading woodland conservation charity, by funding the dedication of trees.

CONTENTS

PARSONAGE HISTORIES: HOUSES, PRIESTS AND PEOPLE

THE PARSON IN the parsonage is one of the perennial features of English life. From medieval village to present-day inner city, via Reformation and Civil War upheavals, elite Georgian comforts, vigorous Victorian reforms and more recent realities and fictions, whether in 'Golden Age' crime stories or the televised struggles of *Rev* in the East End of London in the 2010s, the images are strong. From the Middle Ages to the present day, the houses of local clergy – parsonages, vicarages, rectories and curates' homes – have been amongst the most significant dwellings throughout England. Architecturally they provide some of the best and most fully documented examples of domestic buildings, a widely available way to trace the history of small and medium-sized houses. Locally the parsonage was not just a building but a hub of spiritual and secular activity and links, a place of both change and continuity; it was important for the part it and its occupants have taken in local communities and as a point of connection with the wider world. Parsonages have played a role in many individual and family lives. In public life they have been a key point of contact with national and outside institutions, both spiritual and secular, as they have attempted to transmit authority and influence to local communities.

What is a parsonage? The word is a useful portmanteau term, but confusingly may be used in different ways. Within it lurk a number of important distinctions, and two main meanings. First, 'the parsonage' is the building where the

Opposite: The quintessential English country rectory? Rampisham, Dorset, designed by Augustus Welby Northmore Pugin, and built between 1845 and 1847.

The Old Vicarage, Methwold, Norfolk, now owned by the Landmark Trust. Many parsonages combine successive extensions and rebuilds. Here a richly detailed and fashionable brick gable end of c. 1500 (with later sash windows) is attached to an earlier, medieval timber-framed range.

priest lives in order to exercise spiritual responsibility for the local faithful. The ideal of a resident pastor was an intrinsic part of the development of the English parish from its beginnings. Second, 'parsonage' indicates the ecclesiastical living or benefice of which the clergy house was just one part. The parsonage may be a rectory or a vicarage or a perpetual curacy, and is made up of a house and some combination of land, rights to local ecclesiastical taxes, principally tithes, offerings and fees paid by parishioners – in short, a collection of rights and income. These endowments varied greatly in value from poor to rich, whilst the parishes whose ministry they were originally intended to support also differed in area and population. It is no surprise then that parsonage houses, and the lifestyle of their occupants, could also vary greatly from place to place and region to region. Their links with the surrounding locality were economic and legal as well as spiritual, and closely tied to patterns of patronage. Ownership of the advowson, the right to present an incumbent, determined which priest should hold the living.

This mesh of areas, property rights, legalities and patronage has stayed with church structures since the Middle Ages and continues to provide a necessary parsonage vocabulary. It reflects a medieval system that by the 1530s had covered England in some 8,800 parishes. At its high-water mark, after Victorian expansion, the number of parishes reached over 14,000. Each should have had a parsonage. Also (although they lie outside the scope of this book) we should add the non-Anglican clergy houses that emerged as Protestant Nonconformists and Roman Catholics gained, first, rights to worship (in 1689 and 1791 respectively) and then full civil rights (in 1828 and 1829 respectively). England's landscapes have many thousands of clergy houses that can be explored not only as buildings, but also as part of wider religious and social settings. Some good examples are the grouping of the medieval rectory, manor-house-like, alongside church and barn; or that Victorian triumvirate of influence, the newly built church, alongside a parsonage and school. Each speaks of the continuing but changing roles of the parsonage. As Alan Savidge, an earlier historian of the English parsonage, wrote in 1964, it has been successively 'a hovel, a cottage, a house, a gentleman's residence, a priest's headquarters, the hub of the village … [and now] a problem'.

This book brings together architectural and historical perspectives on English clergy houses. It uses the evidence of buildings, official documents, private records, literary accounts and contemporary and modern images to build a picture of parsonages and their occupants. It also includes a section on tracing the history of a parsonage.

The parsonage as part of a classic grouping with church and school, here newly built in the mid-nineteenth century at Studley, Wiltshire. (Wiltshire Council; Local Studies Collection)

SETTING THE PATTERN: MEDIEVAL PRIESTS' HOUSES

BEGINNINGS

PARSONAGES FIRST APPEAR during the Middle Ages. They were an essential part of the network of parishes that, by the late twelfth or early thirteenth century, had developed to cover most of England. Each parish had a church and a defined area within whose boundaries the parish priest should exercise cure of souls, bringing the sacraments of the church to each inhabitant, from birth to death. The parish was in turn part of a wider ecclesiastical hierarchy, of rural deanery, archdeaconry and diocesan bishopric and, beyond that, archbishop and pope. These authorities increasingly sought to determine what ministry the parish priest should provide, and to ensure that he had the means (the living or benefice) to do so. A suitable house amidst his flock was a key component, together with sufficient income to maintain it during his incumbency. For this period of office the priest enjoyed 'parson's freehold', that is, the right to use the parsonage (the house and the income from the endowment of the living). This typically consisted of glebe, a landholding within the parish; tithes collectable from parishioners; and customary offerings, most often a mortuary on the death of a parishioner, gifts at the main festivals of the church year and fees at burials, marriages and churchings, but not christenings.

Once his incumbency ended, the parson had no further rights in the parsonage. Benefices were treated as pieces of real estate, a collection of rights and income. In this way

Opposite: The medieval parsonage and church at Muchelney, Somerset. The vicarage was ordained by the Bishop of Bath and Wells in 1308, and a new house was built to accommodate the priest (see pages 18–21).

the church was seeking to separate parishes from secular control and notions of inherited lay or clerical interests. This was a major shift from the origins of many local churches. As England was Christianised from the seventh century its early local churches were minsters, serving large hinterlands or *parochiae* from a central church with a group of secular, non-monastic priests. Only gradually did smaller, more local churches develop, their number growing in the tenth and eleventh centuries. This caused the larger parishes of many minster churches to be eroded and divided, although some retained vestiges of their former status, such as rights to bury the dead from their former parochial area.

The origin of the new local churches is seldom documented. Some may have been the collective effort of groups of local people. More often they appear to have been lordly initiatives, beginning as the places of worship of leading local landholders and their tenants, and it was these families who initially owned the majority of the churches that became parish churches. As new and old systems of ecclesiastical and lay authority intermixed, so issues arose, for example who should exercise patronage and control of the advowson, the right to determine which priest should be presented to a local living. The result was a complex and uneven framework of parishes and parsonages, much of it laid down in the twelfth and thirteenth centuries, then inherited through succeeding centuries, and with vestiges persisting today.

The total number and value of churches in the parish system is known from two nationwide surveys. In 1291 and 1292 Edward I, on the authority of Pope Nicholas IV, had listed churches, cathedrals and monasteries in England. This *Taxatio Ecclesiastica* records 8,085 churches and 457 chapelries (dependent, sub-parochial areas with their own churches and clergy but no independent living). A second listing, regarded by historians as more reliable, is the *Valor Ecclesiasticus* of 1535, made for Henry VIII. This records 8,838 parish churches

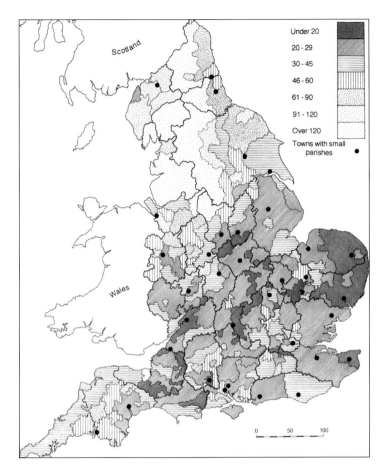

The size distribution of parishes in England (in acres and based on the average parish size in each hundred, wapentake or ward). This map helps explain the varying concentrations and settings of parsonages. (From N. J. G. Pounds, *A History of the English Parish*, Cambridge University Press, 2000)

and 536 chapelries. Despite possible omissions and detailed discrepancies, these surveys provide the best indication of the number and location of parishes and likely parsonages. They also confirm great variations in the size, population and wealth of livings, differences that may reflect origins (as minster or local churches), ownership, geography, population levels or settlement topography. Upland, moorland and marshland places with relatively sparse populations, dispersed settlement and limited economic potential tended to have large parishes. This was particularly apparent in the north of England, where, as noted in the 1821 national census, parishes were on average

The Old Vicarage, Steventon, Oxfordshire (formerly Berkshire), probably built for Robert du Plecy, vicar 1330–57. The west wing (on the right) is of that date. The present hall range and east wing were built after 1557. Like most parsonages before the late seventeenth century, it follows local vernacular building styles.

seven to eight times the size of those in southern counties. Such large parishes tended to be subdivided into chapelries and related townships. Cornwall had more chapelries than parish churches. By contrast, more densely populated areas of the country, with more settlements and more manorial centres, tended to have more early churches and more parishes. Rural parishes here mostly covered less than 500 acres. At each extreme of the spectrum parishes varied in size, from Whalley in north Lancashire at 106,395 acres and with at one point seventeen chapelries, to urban parishes as small as 5 acres. The size, building, lifestyle and maintenance of parsonages varied too, with the living's status as rectory or vicarage one possible determinant.

PARSONAGE: RECTORY OR VICARAGE?

The distinction between a rectory and a vicarage was a result of appropriation, a process that diverted all or part of a church's income to a religious house, other institution or (more rarely) a senior cleric. Most local churches were endowed at an early stage by their lay owners with a glebe, tithes and offerings, which supported the incumbent priest or rector. From the eleventh and twelfth century such endowments were increasingly being given to monastic houses or other bodies such as colleges and hospitals, usually by piously motivated laymen whose ancestors had built churches on their estates. This process considerably profited the recipient institutions, who were now rectors of the appropriated parishes. This left the question of how the local parishioners would be provided for.

From the 1150s reforming bishops strove to control appropriation and, where they approved it, to ensure an adequate house and income for a resident vicar (legally, a substitute for the rector). When a vicarage was ordained the rectors might be required to pay a stipend to the resident vicar, but a more typical provision was that the rector kept the principal income of the great tithes (one tenth of the primary crops, corn, hay and wood) whilst the vicar was provided with a suitable house and a package, usually drawing on income from glebe, lesser tithes (collected from other crops, young animals, profits from activities such as trade, milling and fisheries) and certain offerings and fees from parishioners. Surviving specifications of vicarages reveal the potentially difficult relationship created between parsons and their parishioners. Priests had to be tax collectors and farmers as well as pastors. They were dependent on their flock for an income based on exactions that were complicated to collect and potentially unpopular. This was particularly true of tithes, which remained a source of dispute and sometimes confrontation into the twentieth century. Parsons also needed to farm their glebe or rent it to lessees. Not all takeovers by appropriation resulted in formal vicarages. Some rectors hired a stipendiary chaplain or sent one of their own members to provide 'cure of souls'. After the Reformation this resulted in perpetual curacies, served by relatively poorly paid priests whilst the appropriator controlled all the parish's endowments.

Appropriation was widespread in medieval England, Wales and Scotland. Its tentacles could be far-reaching, with monastic or collegiate rectors distant from their parishes.

Appropriations continued up to the Reformation. The *Valor Ecclesiasticus* of 1535 shows that 37 per cent of English parishes were appropriated. This average hides a wider range of experience. Northern dioceses had high rates of appropriation – Durham (61 per cent), York (53 per cent) and Carlisle (49 per cent), compared with Norwich (25 per cent), Peterborough (26 per cent) and London (28 per cent). Local analysis reveals the impact of appropriation most clearly. Norfolk, one of the most intensively churched of all counties, had 37 per cent of its parishes taken over, with thirty-three appropriating institutions in Norfolk and some twenty elsewhere in England or abroad. For example, Norfolk livings were acquired by monastic houses at Battle in Sussex, Lilleshall in Staffordshire and Longueville in Normandy. Appropriation also affected urban parishes; five in Thetford and twenty-three in Norwich. Some parishes were coveted because of their value. Of thirty-four Norfolk vicarages studied by David Dymond, their average value before appropriation according to the 1291 *taxatio* was £26 against a county average of under £13. After appropriation the vicars of these thirty-four churches were left with an average income of £7, below the county average. It is no surprise that appropriations caused controversy regarding their impact on the church's ministry, draining resources from the parishes and arguably leading to absenteeism, pluralism or other abuses of patronage. They were the butt of some of the most stinging attacks on the worldly greed of the institutional church in the increasingly critical climate of the fourteenth and fifteenth centuries. Yet what the medieval parson in his local parsonage was supposed to do was in theory very clear.

THE LIFE OF THE PARSON AND PARSONAGE

The bishops and archbishops, who ordained clergy and licensed them to specific livings and duties, increasingly laid out generic and consistent requirements, reflected in contemporary manuals. William of Pagula became vicar of Winkfield (Berkshire) in 1314. His guide to priestly duties, *Oculus Sacerdotis,* appeared in the mid-1320s and draws on the instructions of the hierarchy combined with his own parish experience. It shows the ideal of the parson involved at every stage of his parishioners' lives, ensuring immediate baptism, early confirmation (if possible before the child reached five years old), safeguarding sexual morality, marriage and legitimacy, visiting the sick, and providing extreme unction, leading them to penitent deaths followed by the full rites of Christian burial and remembrance of souls.

From birth to death; local clergy at work, seen on the late fifteenth-century seven sacrament font at Great Glemham, Suffolk. By this date both priest and assistant clergy were involved. Here, at baptism, the clerk holds the book for the priest.

The parson's work was marked by an annual round of formal teaching (although, until the later Middle Ages, little preaching). Four times a year he was to instruct his flock in six points: the Articles of Faith, Commandments, Works of Mercy, Deadly Sins, Virtues and Sacraments. Special emphasis was placed on a minimum individual Lenten confession to the priest and subsequent penance. More generally, the parson should give alms to the poor, mediate in local disputes, guard against tyrannies of the powerful in the community, protect the rights of the church in land, property and tithes, ensure reverence for the church building and churchyard, and maintain the vicarage and its hospitality.

The parson's was a pivotal role and a demanding job description. By the thirteenth century the need for a separate dwelling for the priest, where his parishioners knew they could find him and seek his help at any time, was recognised as essential. Here he was now expected to lead a celibate life. Clerical chastity had been enjoined since the eleventh century,

Holy unction; the priest anoints the head of the sick or dying parishioner, while his assistant holds the chrismatory containing the holy oils. A scene from the seven sacrament font at Great Glemham.

both for spiritual reasons and to protect church property rights, which might be threatened by the claims of clerical offspring. Various episcopal visitations reveal that 'hearth companions' and concubines were not easily eliminated from medieval priestly households, but they were suppressed; by the thirteenth century continuing clerical families all but disappeared, in England if not in Wales.

However, the parson did not work or live alone. The growing elaboration of the liturgy and the priest's duties meant that he needed help. Robert Grosseteste, Bishop of Lincoln (1235–53), laid down that if possible there should be a deacon and subdeacon, but 'failing this, at least a suitable and honourable clerk to serve the priest during the divine offices'. Such clerks figure often, probably local men in minor orders, perhaps young and training for priesthood. The clerk sang and made responses at services, read the epistle and served the priest at mass, cleaned the church, prepared the vestments, books, candles, wine, holy water, incense and oils, laundered linen, rang the bells, went with the priest on sick visits, dug graves and kept keys. So parishes increasingly expected not just a single clergyman but the parson and one or more assistants. A minority of medieval parish clergy were graduates and there was no universal pattern of training or level of literacy. There were men of noble and gentrified background amongst the clergy, more often in non-parochial roles or the richest livings, but the parson as theologically trained scholar and gentleman was a figure still far ahead. The majority of medieval parochial clergy in the largest English diocese, Lincoln, were serving within 20 miles of their homes and had been ordained in the same diocese.

MEDIEVAL PARSONAGES: THE BUILDINGS

Although there were thousands of medieval parsonages, very few original buildings now remain. As religious, social and economic circumstances and expectations changed, so early parsonages were widely superseded. Medieval structures were demolished, turned to other roles from manor house to school to subdivided labourers' housing, or incorporated (as here at Market Deeping) into rebuilt rectories or vicarages. Surviving buildings, supplemented by contemporary documents and occasional archaeological evidence, provide some clues.

Appropriated rectories had the richest clergy houses. At Ashleworth in Gloucestershire the manor and church were both owned by the Augustinian St Augustine's Abbey, Bristol. As lords and rectors the abbey created a complex of buildings by the River Severn. The archetypal manor house (with classic plan of central hall, until the seventeenth century open to the roof, upper and lower chambers at the north end and another chamber over service rooms at the south end) stands with the demesne farm, large storage barns and the church. Much of

The Old Rectory, Market Deeping, Lincolnshire. The medieval parsonage comprises a hall house with many additions. The garden front was remodelled in 1832 in Gothic style, displaying the family arms of the then incumbent, Reverend W. Hildyard.

the building dates from the fifteenth century, representing a significant investment by the abbey at a time when the rectory and its manor were leased to improving lay tenants.

Lower down the parsonage scale were vicarage houses. At Muchelney, a natural island amidst the marshlands of Somerset, the rare surviving medieval priest's house demonstrates the workings of an appropriated living in an unusually direct way (see page 8). The major Benedictine abbey, with its 250-foot-long church and extensive claustral buildings, stands next to

the parish church of St Peter and St Paul, across the road from which is the original vicarage house. The abbey took over the church but did not ordain a vicarage, instead sending someone from the abbey to conduct services for the parishioners. In 1308 the Bishop of Bath and Wells intervened to ensure a formal appropriation, ordaining a vicarage. The provision for the vicar in this case could be partly in kind, given the short distance to the abbey's kitchens. He was brought a large loaf and two gallons of ale daily, with a dish of meat on Sundays and Tuesdays and eggs or fish on other days.

The vicar of Muchelney in Somerset received food and drink from the nearby Muchelney Abbey, a link perhaps portrayed in this carving (found on the abbey site) of a monk carrying bread and ale.

A new vicarage house with garden and orchard was built, in local stone, with cruck timbers and a thatched roof. It is rectangular in plan, with a central hall originally open to the roof and a screens passage, with to the west a buttery or service room with a chamber above. To the east of the hall is a parlour with the unheated priest's chamber above it. The two upstairs chambers were originally reached by staircase turrets at either end of the building. Early sixteenth-century modifications brought comforts characteristic of the widespread sixteenth- and seventeenth-century rebuilding of vernacular houses. A floor was inserted, turning the hall into two storeys. The fine fireplace in the hall, with its great lintel of local Ham stone, was installed.

Muchelney vicarage shows appropriation at work and is typical of medieval vicarage buildings on a par with the vernacular houses of prosperous peasant farmers or yeomen. Muchelney vicarage also demonstrates the fluctuating fortunes that could beset parsonage houses. After the Reformation the vicarage saw vacancies, use as a school, decay of the fabric,

Plan of the ground floor of the Priest's House, Muchelney (after Platt). A staircase (later removed) led to the upper chamber for the priest at the east end. The full-height hall allowed no direct communication between the priest's and domestic quarters at the west end.

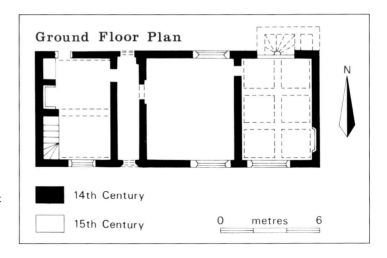

Ground Floor Plan

■ 14th Century

□ 15th Century

0   metres   6

N

and failure to meet changing expectations of a suitable clergy house, culminating in it being labelled in the nineteenth century as an inconvenient cottage. Unusually it was rescued, after being reported to the Society for the Protection of Ancient Buildings as likely to be demolished. Bought by the National Trust, it was restored from 1911 to 1912 by those leading figures of the Arts and Crafts Movement, Ernest Barnsley and Norman Jewson.

Documents recording the provision of vicarage houses in the aftermath of appropriation provide some of the earliest detailed descriptions of medieval parsonages. The Benedictine monks of Eynsham Abbey, Oxfordshire, agreed that a house should be built by 1268 for the vicar of their church at Histon, Cambridgeshire. The new vicarage was to be constructed of good oak timbers, with a hall at least 26 feet by 20 feet, with a buttery at one end and at the other a 'competent' chamber with a garderobe. There was also to be a kitchen, bakehouse and brewhouse, probably in a separate building.

At Chalgrove in Oxfordshire the church had been given by the king to the Cistercian abbey of Thame, which thus became its rector. Within two years, in 1319, the diocesan bishop of Lincoln had ordained a vicarage there. The vicar

was to have a cottage on one acre of land in the middle of the village, and with two acres of land and one acre of meadow belonging to it and free of secular exactions and services. The house was to be rebuilt by Easter to provide a new hall and two

The Priest's House, Muchelney, from the north-east, showing the exterior of the first-floor priest's chamber, and the elaborate windows added in the fifteenth century.

Ordaining a new vicarage; a detailed description for Chalgrove, Oxfordshire, in the register of the Bishop of Lincoln for 1319.

rooms, one for the vicar and the other 'for guests happening to come'. The vicarage also had a small close, a stable, kitchen and brewhouse. The vicar's living would be drawn from fees, offerings and some limited tithes. The abbey would provide two cartloads of good hay each year, and initially find books, vestments and ecclesiastical ornaments for the vicar. After that the vicar would have to maintain these means of worship himself and provide a chaplain for the dependent chapelry of Berrick. Until the rebuilt vicarage was completed, the priest was to live in 'the principal dwelling house of the church itself', that is, the original rectory now owned by the abbey. Chalgrove, like other appropriated parishes, ended up with both rectory and vicarage buildings.

This was generally thought appropriate but some vicars and additional clergy, assistants or chaplains were allocated a share of the existing rectory house. When in 1349 the Benedictine nuns of Bungay appropriated Redenhall in Norfolk, a wall had to be built across the parsonage to separate the vicar's part from the rector's (i.e. the nunnery's). More often rectors wished to use their property uninterrupted, with the vicar's role clearly distinct. At West Harptree in Somerset, appropriated to the Augustinian abbey of Keynsham, the bishop ordained in 1344 that the vicar have use of 'all the houses of the rectory with the dovecote, curtilage and garden adjacent', but only as a temporary expedient because the bishop thought that the priest should 'have a house separate from the houses of the rectory and nearer to the church'. This was achieved by allocating a tenanted property opposite the gates of the rectory. This was 'fitting for the status of the vicar', having a curtilage (adjoining land), close and a hall with solars and cellars at either end. A kitchen, granary, stable for three horses and a dovecote were to be built within six months. The vicar was also to have 5 acres of arable land, two of meadow, free common pasture in the fields and hills and freedom to cut heath in the hills of Mendip.

Clearly there was significant new building or rebuilding of parsonage houses during the Middle Ages, with substantial, submanorial vernacular homes regarded as the appropriate norm. Local materials were used and hall houses, with ground-floor rooms with upper chambers to either side of the open hall were common. These were not family households but could accommodate the priest, who had a private room, his assistants and servants, and guests. Hall houses were not found everywhere. Clerical tower houses appear in the north of England as at Newton Arlosh in Cumbria, where the abbot of Holm Cultram was authorised to build a new church in 1304. The result was this hefty combination of church and defensible tower for the priest, with a fireplace and garderobe on the first floor. It follows the pattern of pele towers elsewhere in what was inhospitable and unstable border territory. Other northern

Newton Arlosh, Cumbria, a new church authorised in 1304. The parsonage is a defensible tower house, following the pattern of clerical pele towers in the unsettled Borders, but here attached to the church.

West Dean,
East Sussex, an
austere stone
parsonage of the
late thirteenth
century. It has a
single entrance
and two principal
floors, each
with a large and
a small room
and heated
with a fireplace,
probably to
accommodate
more than
one priest.

tower houses for priests include the vicar's pele at Corbridge, perhaps as late as the fourteenth century and with single rooms on first and second floors; and Elsdon Tower, both in Northumberland. Substantial austerity was not confined to the north, as the late thirteenth-century parsonage at West Dean in East Sussex suggests. However, in less threatened and more prosperous areas, it seems that houses like Muchelney became more typical as parsonages. The houses of urban clergy are less well known. They are likely to have occupied houses in the general local style, on burgage plots or in terraces. Identifiable medieval town parsonages tend not to survive, being superseded by later buildings.

Archaeology may help indicate early and changed parsonages, although firm identification is difficult. Wharram Percy in the East Yorkshire Wolds is a deserted village with manorial complex, church and parsonage, as well as peasant houses and was excavated between 1950 and 1990. Its deserted state allowed it to be subject to uniquely intensive investigation. Settlement developed from the tenth to the twelfth centuries. The ruins of the parish church of St Martin are one of the few features still remaining above ground. Excavation suggests that the original site of the parsonage probably lay on the southern edge of the churchyard, a typical village house with accompanying plot. After the church was given by the Percy lords of the manor to the recently founded Augustinian priory at Haltemprice near Hull in 1327, the new rectors seem to have replanned the site, building a new parsonage to the north of the church across a roadway leading to the churchyard. The house was part of a working farming complex. It was subject to fire and rebuilding, but continued despite depopulation of the village for sheep grazing, the last tenants leaving between 1488 and 1506. The eighteenth-century parsonage was a long, vernacular thatched house, with three rooms and a pantry in line. It was to be described, in that increasingly familiar Victorian style, as a mean cottage, unfitting for a modern parson. Wharram Percy is a good example of the building and rebuilding and sometimes re-siting to which parsonages were subject. It also shows how the ecclesiastical arrangements set in the early Middle Ages became fixed, persisting despite changes in population and settlement.

Wharram Percy, East Yorkshire – a reconstruction of the church and priest's house of this deserted medieval village. Surviving early parsonages are rare; here, archaeological excavation suggests the form of the parsonage, shown as a peasant-style house to the south of the churchyard.

Late medieval
changes; the
Luttrell Psalter,
made in England
in the 1330s, has
many images of
a world turned
upside down.
This grotesque
creature has the
upper body of
a pilgrim; the
badge on his hat
is upside down,
questioning the
validity of his
pilgrimage.

LATE MEDIEVAL PARSONS AND PARSONAGES

Parish life changed and developed significantly in the fourteenth and fifteenth centuries. In the words of the historian Dorothy Owen, by the end of the Middle Ages 'the parish church had evolved from a territorial chapel dependent on a local landowner, and controlled by him and his priest, into a shrine, meeting place, and possession of all the parishioners'. The position of the priest in this community of the parish was different from that in the thirteenth century. Then the church in England reached a peak of spiritual drive and institutional influence, wealth and organised power. Now direct and indirect pressures, both material and spiritual, challenged that authority. There were internal disruptions, including the Papal Schism (1378–1418) with rival popes in Rome and Avignon. External factors, population pressure, war, inflation and high taxes and agricultural difficulties brought secular stresses that made the maintenance of the church's income more difficult and, in the eyes of some, more questionable. Then came the catastrophe of the Black Death, in the initial outbreak of which (1348–9) a third to a half of the English population died. Many clergy perished and the numbers and quality of local priests declined at a time when the church's exactions, now from fewer people, did not.

Anti-clericalism was a significant strand in the Peasants' Revolt of 1381, during which Archbishop Sudbury of Canterbury was executed by the rebels, amongst whose leaders was John Ball, an excommunicate priest. The presence of large numbers of unbeneficed clergy, poor and unconnected to patronage and preferment, made for resentful voices. The late fourteenth century also saw the first English heresy, Lollardy, articulated by a scholar priest, John Wycliffe; its emphasis was on access for the laity to the Bible in English, and criticism of the church's wealth, of monasticism, pilgrimages and other practices.

This changed and uncertain context led not to a rejection of faith by English parishioners, but to an active lay piety and intervention in local church life. Church buildings changed, with enlarged naves and aisles and chapels. New endowments, grand and small, provided for chantries, guilds, fraternities and memorial masses, services often requiring the appointment of clergy in addition to the parish priest. Increasing lay authority in the running of the parish was seen in the development of the office of churchwarden as guardian of the cemetery, the church building, its furnishings and property. What these trends meant for clergy housing can be seen in the case of Long Melford in Suffolk.

Long Melford's magnificent parish church was remodelled in the late fifteenth century and is a graphic expression of late medieval lay piety, display and communal effort in a small town prospering from farming, its market and cloth making.

Long Melford, Suffolk – a fine example of the development of late medieval parish life. The church was substantially rebuilt in the late fifteenth century. The neighbouring parsonage (left) was a much later addition to the parochial group.

The parish was big, at 5,185 acres, with two chapels of ease, each a mile from the church. Long Melford was a wealthy rectory. From late Saxon times its main manor and the church benefice were owned by Bury St Edmunds Abbey, although it was never formally appropriated and no vicarage was ordained. The fifteenth-century church had seven altars, forty-four copes and forty-six liturgical books and contained several private, enclosed chantry chapels, served by specially appointed priests and with endowments administered by trustees or feoffees. There were provisions also for trentals (sets of thirty commemorative masses), obits (annual recreations of funerals) and sangreds (public reminders to pray for the souls of named individuals). Late medieval Long Melford also had at least six guildhalls and other property bequeathed to the parish, including, by 1537, almshouses.

The multiplication of church buildings and clergy housing in the late Middle Ages can be seen here at Long Melford, Suffolk.

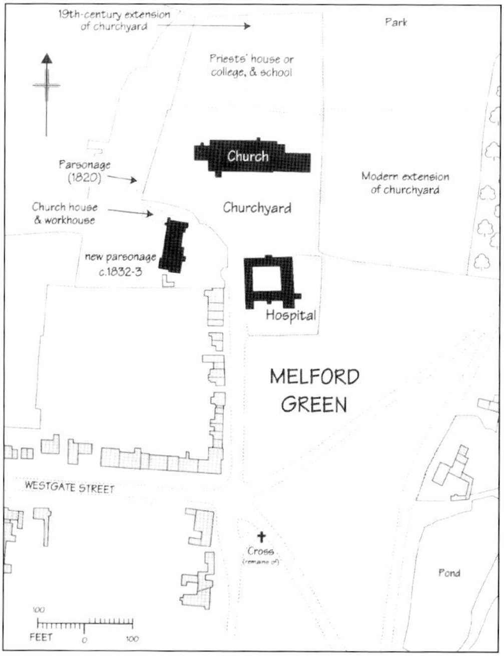

On the churchyard's north edge was the priests' house or college, a private house used partly as a school and partly adapted as accommodation for the chantry and other unbeneficed clergy now needed to serve the parish church. By the south-west corner of the churchyard was the church house, owned by the parish and used for social events involving eating, drinking, music and dancing, valuable sources of income but now considered inappropriate in the church itself. Away from the church were the two chapelries and the original parsonage or rectory house, a mile to the west, part of the glebe estate, operating as a separate manor. The medieval

19th-century extension of churchyard

Park

Priests' house or college, & school

Church

Parsonage (1820)

Modern extension of churchyard

Church house & workhouse

Churchyard

new parsonage c.1832-3

Hospital

MELFORD GREEN

WESTGATE STREET

Cross (remains of)

Pond

FEET   0   100

Gipping, a separate medieval chapelry in the parish of Stowmarket, Suffolk. The church was built for Sir James Tyrell, lord of the manor, in the 1480s. The north chapel (now vestry), with blocked windows and fireplace, may have housed the chaplain.

rectory and separate priests' house by the church continued beyond the Reformation. Only after 1750 were three successive rectories of increasing grandeur built at the south-west corner of the churchyard, bringing together the main parsonage and church. Long Melford's experience shows how early history can determine the building and location of the parsonage, its status as rectory or vicarage, and how additional clergy housing and church buildings might develop as parish and priestly roles changed later in the Middle Ages.

A rare surviving example of a chantry priest's house-cum-almshouse at Fyfield, Oxfordshire (formerly Berkshire), built in the early fifteenth century. The priest lived in the west wing (to the left). The building is now a pub.

In Chancery.

Between ye Warden and Brethren of ye Hospital
Hospital the Holy & blessed Trinity of ye foundation
of Sr Wm Cordall Kn{t} in Melford ———— Compl{ts}

James Johnson Clerk ———————— Def{t}

This Book was produced & shewn to Mrs Martha Bisbie upon her
examination to the fourteenth Interr{y} on the part of ye Compl{ts} this sixteenth
day of Octobr One thousand seven hundred and thirty six Before us

Fouldes   Jos: Grigby,   Matt: Unwin

Melford Parsonage

or

An account touchinge the Rents, Tithes,
and profits thereof; as they were received
by Nathaniel Bisbie D.D. duringe his
beinge Incumbent, and Rector there: written out of his papers and yearly accounts
with his owne hand; and reduced by him:
for the better method, and continued remembrance of the same into this volume.
Witness his hand this second day of Au-
gust. anno Dni 1676.

Nath: Bisbie.

THE POST-REFORMATION PARSONAGE

PARSONAGES IN THE sixteenth and seventeenth centuries were caught up in enormous changes, national in scope but realised, sometimes painfully, at parish level from the 1530s. Firstly, parsonages were a key component in the establishment of a Protestant reformed state church, which brought institutional and political changes, spiritual shifts in hearts and minds, and married clergy to parsonages. Secondly, with the dissolution of the monasteries many parsonages, both houses and livings, found their way into lay ownership. Thirdly, also beginning in the 1530s, the Tudors were adopting the parish as their basic unit of local government, investing it with a comprehensive range of responsibilities to produce a dual civil and ecclesiastical parish system that was to persist until the 1830s. The parson in the parsonage was becoming more central in local society, but in a very different context.

The Reformation and its fierce aftershocks directly affected individual parishes. It left the English permanently divided in matters of religion, fissures that were harshly apparent in the next century through civil war, interregnum, and restoration of the monarchy and the Church of England in 1660. After the institutional break with Rome of Henry VIII's reign, more radical religious and liturgical change came under Edward VI (1547–53), including the dissolution of chantries, the first and second Acts of Uniformity and Books of Common Prayer, and the prohibition of images and vestments. The succession of Mary I (1553–8) brought a brief return to Catholic worship.

Opposite: After the Restoration of the monarchy and the Church of England in 1660, the clergy collected records and created new accounts of parsonage rights and property with added zeal, as witnessed here in the Reverend Dr Nathaniel Bisbie's book *Melford Parsonage* (see page 39). He was rector of Long Melford in Suffolk from 1660 to 1690.

The impact of religious change and differences is mirrored in the contrasting dress of groups and individuals at this feast in Bermondsey, painted by Jovis Hoefnagel c. 1569. Plain, dark, puritan restraint and rich, colourful display are both in evidence.

Only after Elizabeth I became queen in 1558 did a new church settlement, Act of Uniformity and reintroduction of a revised Book of Common Prayer suggest a middle way, which was intended to provide a shared route to religious conformity and loyal citizenship for all Elizabeth's subjects. Many local parsonages experienced upheaval and uncertainty. For example, in 1554 in Ely diocese 20 per cent of priests were deprived of their livings, mostly because they were married. The rural north-Oxfordshire parish of Swalcliffe had no fewer than four vicars between 1554 and 1559, the last of whom, Robert Wood, was deprived of his living in 1559 at the time of the reimposition of the Book of Common Prayer.

The unity of the Elizabethan Church of England was strained, with recusant Roman Catholics and some Protestants, who chose a separatist route and often exile, remaining outside it. Amongst the majority remaining in the fold there was a wide spectrum, from Calvinist Puritan godly to High Church

Arminians, differences that became increasingly clear under the assertive leadership of the royalist Archbishop Laud of Canterbury in the 1630s. The different camps were apparent in and out of church, in everything from theology and liturgy to church furnishing, leisure pursuits, clothing and lifestyle.

It was an uncomfortable time to be a parson in a parish where your churchmanship did not match that of the parishioners. Dr John Manby, a Laudian, became rector of Cottenham, a rich living in Cambridgeshire worth £500 a year, in 1635. The patron of the living was the bishop, and Manby had married the bishop's daughter. The parish was Puritan. Manby was accused of ceremonial worship and refusing to read Parliamentary proclamations in church. Eventually he and his wife and five young children were forcibly ejected from the rectory, their dinner gobbled up by their persecutors and everyone afraid to give them shelter. Although restored to Cottenham from 1660 to 1671, Manby's daughter recalled how 'the children were soe full of hatred, takeing it from their parents', that they refused to play with the rectory children. Parsonage life, so often an existence apart, now also affected the wives and children of a married clergy. It is estimated that some 30 per cent of English livings were under sequestration at some time between 1643 and 1660, and that 20 per cent of Restoration clergy were ejected in 1662. Amongst these nonconformists were some of the leaders of the dissenting churches, which now began to take root in English towns and countryside.

As we have seen, during the Middle Ages rectories and vicarages and the rights to present clergy to them had been appropriated on a large scale to monasteries and other corporate bodies. That medieval system was preserved after the Reformation but, particularly with the dissolution of the monasteries in the 1530s, ex-monastic property was extensively granted or sold by the Crown to new owners, mostly laymen. Sometimes ecclesiastical property stayed in church or collegiate hands. For example, Ashleworth rectoral manor and church living were granted in 1542 to the newly created diocese of Bristol. Swalcliffe, granted in the 1380s by the Bishop of Winchester as part of the initial endowment to his New College, Oxford, remained in the college's hands, with a modest vicarage house alongside the college's grand rectoral manor house, tithe barn and church. More typical was the change that took place at Long Melford. There the rich, late medieval world of the parish church, its images and annual round of rituals, its chantries and multiple priests, was dismantled. Bury St Edmunds Abbey was supplanted as the main property owner by Sir William Cordell, a career lawyer who acquired the main manor and the advowson of the rectory. It was he who, in 1573, founded the hospital, an almshouse for twelve poor men, on the churchyard's south edge. Ownership, responsibility and leadership were shifting in a world now with many lay tithe owners, lay rectors or lay impropriators (as lay successors to ecclesiastical appropriators were legally known).

The system of local government developed by the Tudors was rooted in the parish or (in the larger parishes) its subdivisions, townships. The functions of parish government were numerous. From 1538 the parson and churchwarden were directed by the king to jointly keep registers of baptisms, marriages and burials. Increasingly, the parish was also charged with the relief and control of poverty. To this was added maintenance of highways, providing men for the militia and (if the manorial court was inactive) management of communal agriculture. The parish was given extensive responsibilities for reporting to higher authorities: on law and order, sedition and recusancy to the quarter-session courts, and on the church fabric, religious conformity, sexual conduct and much more to the archdeacon. The parish vestry of ratepayers, with the incumbent as *ex officio* chairman, annually elected parish officers – churchwardens, overseers of the poor, constable, highways surveyor and others – to fulfil these roles. The vestry could raise rates for parish needs and was also expected to

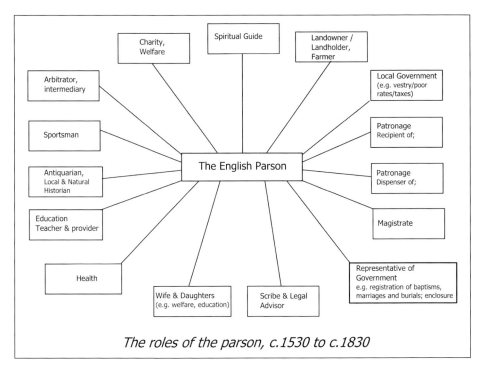

The roles of the parson, c.1530 to c.1830

collect certain county and national taxes. Parish government was an encompassing system in which church and state, parson and people were inextricably and constantly involved in a wide range of secular and social concerns and contacts. Its growth played a major part in putting the parson and parsonage at the hub of local activities and relationships.

But post-Reformation parish life was not only a matter of government, politics or property. This was also the period when the ideal pattern of post-Reformation ministry was spelt out in a work of lasting influence, *A Priest to the Temple or The Country Parson, His Character, and Rule of Holy Life* by the priest and poet George Herbert (1593–1633). Written in his rectory in the village of Bemerton, Wiltshire, in 1632, it was published posthumously in 1652. For Herbert the parsons' purpose, as 'deputies of Christ', was to bring all their flock to a knowledge and obedience of God. The parson should

The parsonage was at the hub of local church and secular life as the priest fulfilled many roles and expectations, especially between the 1530s and 1830s.

George Herbert (1593–1633), rector of Bemerton, near Salisbury, and author of an influential guide to the ideal parson and parsonage.

care for his people 'as if he had begot the whole parish', yet this spiritual ideal was attainable only by recognising practical realities, that parishioners would fall out, resent the parson's tithes, sleep in church and be preoccupied with their demanding daily round. Preaching should therefore 'give them stories and sayings they will remember' and relate to the circumstances of their own lives. The parson should be 'not witty, or learned, or eloquent, but Holy', helping them in their daily lives not only as pastor but as lawyer and physician. The parsonage played a key role in realising this ideal, according to Herbert. There the parson's wife raised their children, 'curing and healing all wounds and sores with her own hands', making home-bred medicines from the plants of the parsonage garden. Their children should visit other sick children. Charity and education should be provided. The parsonage servants (the Herberts had six) should be taught to read and write. On the walls of the plain and simply furnished rooms texts should be painted, including 'Who so leadeth a godly life: he shall be my servant'. The rectory doors should be open to the needy. On great festivals none should 'want a good meal suitable to the joy of the occasion'. Cleanliness, a careful diet, and food from their own garden and orchard were touchstones of parsonage life, a self-disciplined existence in which the parson and his flock would recognise his worthiness to bring them to 'heaven in ordinarie'.

Post-Reformation parsonages are better recorded than those before. For example, Ralph Josselin, an Anglican country parson, kept a diary during his time as vicar of Earls Colne, Essex, from 1641 to 1683 which offers rich insights into the realities of parsonage life. An Anglican of Puritan persuasion, he had gone as a chaplain to Cromwell's troops in 1645. His forty-two-year ministry spans the Civil War, Interregnum and Restoration. His diary is both a confessional of individual faith (he writes, 'I find Sathan like the lapwing crying before me with … temptation and vanity') and a record of daily life and ministry. Josselin and his wife, Jane, had ten children in twenty-one years, five predeceasing him. In 1650, as his son Ralph lay dying, aged thirteen months, he wrote, 'Lord thy will be done, thou art better to mee than sonnes and daughters, though I value them above gold and jewels'. His recording of weaning, teething and first steps suggests a loving father and a full and noisy household.

The one room that distinguished parsonages from other houses of this period was the study, a necessary retreat for parsons now expected to deliver a ministry of the word, and to prepare and deliver frequent sermons. As was increasingly the clerical norm, Ralph Josselin was a graduate. The Josselin household experienced the tensions of teenage and young adult angst, all the while striving to find the means to maintain ministry, family and the expected hospitality. The anticipated yearly income of £80 was not always realised. Tithes were collected (shared with the lay impropriator), but not always in full. Only 49 per cent of Josselin's income came from the ecclesiastical living. For the rest land was farmed, leased

The title page of George Herbert's *A Priest to the Temple or The Country Parson*, first published posthumously in 1652.

The church and rectory at Bemerton, where George Herbert wrote *A Priest to the Temple or The Country Parson*.

A map of Long Melford rectory manor in 1613, originally in Nathaniel Bisbie's book.

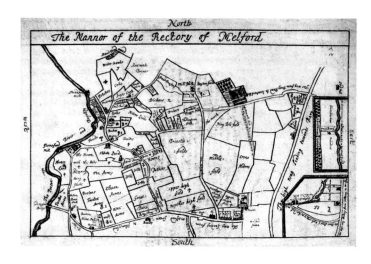

and some sold, and school was taught. The vicarage children went to the village school and became increasingly expensive until they went into trade or service and married. Even as they left home, provision for dowries increased costs. Josselin's household expenditure shows a steady commitment to charity, hospitality and books, but this is considerably outweighed by the costs of farming, of maintaining the parsonage, of Mr and Mrs Josselin and their servants, of family baptisms, marriages and funerals, and particularly of the children.

Personal, estate, church and national records, published histories and surviving buildings all contribute further to the picture. Estate records became fuller, kept by lay owners of parsonages and sometimes by parsons themselves. At Long Melford, Dr Nathaniel Bisbie was appointed rector in 1660 by the lay patron and remained so until 1690. A Restoration

Leicestershire houses and parsonages in 1666, showing the number of hearths in each. (After J. H. Pruett, 1978)

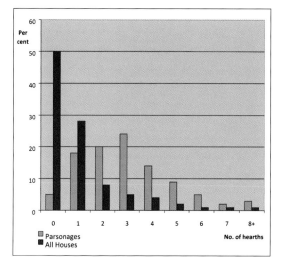

man, he believed that 'every man was restored to his own again' after the misguided years of Civil War and Commonwealth. Determined and litigious, he set out to record in the still-surviving book *Melford Parsonage* past records and present details of the parsonage (see page 30). As rector and lord of the rectory manor he sought to ensure that every right and income was confirmed and enforced.

Bisbie's quest made him what has been called the first historian of Melford. He was not alone. It is no accident that the first parish history published in England appeared in 1695. Its author, White Kennett, was the vicar of Ambrosden, Oxfordshire. His research into local records had begun in order to defend disputed claims to church charity lands. It continued as a quest to maintain 'veneration to the Church of England' and broadened into a full-scale antiquarian local history. He was an early example of the many clerical historians who researched and wrote in their parsonages. A shared early motivation seems to have been to (re)establish the historical continuities and claims of church livings after the huge disruptions between 1642 and 1660.

Parsonages become traceable too in national and church records. National taxes of the 1660s were assessed by number of hearths per house. Local hearth tax returns allow clerical houses to be compared with houses in general. The picture for Stuart Leicestershire shows that nine out of ten parishes had parsonage houses, ranging in size from four-room cottages to twenty-room mansions. Overall parsonages appear in the middle range of size and comfort as indicated by numbers of hearths. This translates, on average, to six to ten rooms.

Two other sources, probate inventories and glebe terriers, may provide detailed accounts of individual parsonages. Probate was governed by church courts until 1858. Inventories of all movable goods of the deceased were required by the courts and those compiled between *c.* 1520 and *c.* 1750 are particularly rich in detail, as local appraisers went room to

The church and vicarage at Steyning, West Sussex, shown in a 1781 watercolour by S. H. Grimm. Increasing evidence regarding parsonage history is available in the post-Reformation period. An inventory of 1643 describes the rooms and contents of Steyning vicarage in detail.

room and into yard and garden to list furnishings, personal belongings, books, tools, crops and stock, debts and credits. A Sussex study of 181 clergy inventories between 1600 and 1750 finds them 'representative of the wider community, ranging from the very lowly and poverty-stricken to the level of county gentry'. Steyning vicarage is amongst them. Its inventory, taken in 1643 on the death of the vicar, Leonard Stalman, reveals a house of eleven rooms – hall, kitchen, parlour, chamber over parlour, two further chambers, study, loft, garret, closet and cellar. Further working rooms, which may be in or outside the main house, were the brewhouse, woodhouse (with cheesepress) and wheat loft. Unusually no barn or stable was listed. Stalman was born in Craven, Yorkshire (clergy were now more likely to be non-locals), a graduate, and married. His goods were worth £116 8s 2d and he left his two grandsons and granddaughter silver vessels in his will. His condition contrasts strikingly with that of the unbeneficed curate of North Stoke, also in Sussex. Thomas Heare died in 1620, his goods worth £4 18s, and his poor home containing empty chests, old sheets, a parcel of old books, a flock bed, some pots, dishes and one pig.

Glebe terriers, church records ordained in 1571 and 1604, are surveys of parish property, collected periodically and

preserved in parish and diocesan records. Most numerous after 1660, they describe the parsonage house, at their most detailed including walling, roofing and flooring materials and naming rooms. Cumberworth parsonage in Lincolnshire is thus described in 1625: '3 bays built all of wood and walled with earth covered with reeds & rushes, 2 bays chambered and boarded over at both ends. 8 rooms – hall, 2 parlours, 2 chambers, buttery, milkhouse, coalhouse. Item one kitchen consisting of 2 bayes.' Detached kitchens were a common medieval feature, a precaution against fire. Glebe terriers show some surviving, but with a trend to kitchens in the main house. Other trends discernible during the seventeenth century are a decline in halls and an increase in parlours and cellars. Terriers may also describe the parson's farmstead, garden, orchard and yard, and wider landholding. The parsonage as working farm most frequently included barns and stables and outbuildings, such as for cattle, pigs, pigeons, meal, chaff, wood or dairy work. Some terriers also itemise the sources of glebe income – tithes, mortuaries, offerings, fees and stipends.

If numbers of glebe terriers survive for the same living then alterations, rebuildings or replacements may be traced, and links made to other documents and ideally to surviving buildings.

Misleading names? The church and Old Rectory at Froxfield, Wiltshire. The rectory was appropriated by Easton Priory in 1396, and passed out of church hands after the dissolution of the monasteries. This rectory was thus not the home of the local parsons, who lived in a separate house, Froxfield Vicarage.

An urban vicarage, in Banbury, Oxfordshire, rebuilt in 1649, still in local vernacular style and material (ironstone).

It may prove that early parsonages did not survive, superseded by later, more prestigious houses; or that they remain, reused in new guises. Unravelling the identity of the 'real' parsonage, especially in a landscape of changed names (Parsonage Farm, or the Manor or the Old Rectory), is an occupational hazard for parsonage historians. Where the link between standing building and documents is clear, much can be understood. The parsonage in the Suffolk town of Eye has twenty terriers, from 1490 to 1908. Relating these to the surviving building, Sylvia Colman has shown how the parsonage grew from a simple two- or three-cell house to a grand dwelling of some twenty rooms, in four ranges and with building phases of 1627, 1723, 1725 and 1845.

By 1700 English parsonages still varied greatly in wealth, size and style. They were essentially vernacular houses, typical of the middle range of local housing, built of the same materials and with similar plans and range of rooms but with the addition of a study. Many were also farmsteads, and the average parsonage has been likened to the average farmhouse, but better documented. During the sixteenth and seventeenth centuries parsonages became a key focus for a changed and extended range of official activities and connections. They were now also family homes. Some were extended in a piecemeal fashion. During the later seventeenth century there were signs of a shift beginning from vernacular to polite styles and to genteel aspiration in the architecture of parsonages. Urban parsonages had also followed local domestic building styles before 1660, as in the vicarage at Banbury, rebuilt in 1649 after Civil War damage. Now new

The medieval vicarage in Burford, Oxfordshire, rebuilt in 1672 but no longer in the vernacular style, as witnessed by the symmetrical façade, shaped gables and first-floor *piano nobile*. In 1836 a new wing and coach-house were added to the rear. It was superseded in 1937 by a smaller, modern vicarage.

styles began to appear, seen in the rebuilt vicarage of 1672 at Burford, Oxfordshire. Rural parsonages were also changing. New work might involve a rebuild or a smart façade, as at Hale, Lancashire (now Cheshire). Here a new incumbent, the Reverend William Langford, remodelled the parsonage in *c.* 1703, adding a classical, five-bay façade of sandstone and brick, a panelled entrance hall and interiors. Behind this lurks a humble, unrebuilt early seventeenth-century section. It is a contrast that prefigures the grandeur associated with the comforts and status of the Georgian parsonage in its prime.

This parsonage in Hale, Cheshire (formerly Lancashire), elegantly rebuilt *c.* 1703, retains more humble early seventeenth-century buildings to the rear. Now no longer a clergy house, it has been renamed The Manor House.

GEORGIAN PARSONAGES: A GOLDEN AGE?

Throughout the Georgian period the English parsonage continued on an ever more gentlemanly trajectory. Widely rebuilt and expanded, sometimes new-built, it grew in architectural politeness and gentility, visually and socially ever more distant from the generality of local society in a way that the vernacular parsonages of earlier periods had seldom been. Thus in the vast parish of Simonburn, in Northumberland north of Hadrian's Wall, the rector of the wealthy living in 1725 built a house of five bays and three storeys, its style evoking that of John Vanbrugh (see page 46). The back-door lintel bears the date of the previous build, 1666, which in turn had replaced a medieval tower house. At Farnborough on the Berkshire downs the rectory was rebuilt in 1749, of five bays and using grey vitrified bricks and red-brick dressings in wholly polite style (see page 3). The Old Rectory at Epworth, Lincolnshire, was rebuilt following a fire in 1709, a catastrophe from which John Wesley, future founder of Methodism, escaped safely (see page 46).

The surroundings as well as the house were significant, as seen at Wilford, Nottinghamshire. Here the rector built a substantial double-pile house in *c.* 1720, setting it in a miniature park through which a drive led to the forecourt overlooking a garden, with barn, stable and coach-house to one side. There was also a summerhouse on the banks of the River Trent. Such expenditure was especially worthwhile in the case of 'family livings', where patronage meant that the parsonage was expected to remain with a member or nominee of the family

Teigh Old Rectory, built in 1740, is a classic example of a grand parsonage adjacent to its church. It was used as Mr Collins' living in the 1995 television adaptation of Jane Austen's *Pride and Prejudice* and now serves as a bed and breakfast.

Parsonages were built and rebuilt in the first half of the eighteenth century in increasingly gentlemanly style, as shown here at Simonburn, Northumberland (1725).

at each change of incumbent. At Farnborough the Price family acquired the advowson *c.* 1720, held it until 1883 and served as rectors. A version of such style, status and comfort became the ideal for a parsonage. Jane Austen, in *Persuasion* (published 1818), describes Uppercross as 'a moderate-sized village … containing only two houses superior in appearance to those

The elegant former rectory at Epworth, Lincolnshire, rebuilt after a fire of 1709.

of the yeoman and labourers – the mansion of the 'squire ... and the compact, tight parsonage, enclosed in its own neat garden, with a vine and a peach tree trained round its casements'.

If this was the ideal parsonage, then Austen, a clergy daughter, was acutely aware that it was not always attainable given the sharp inequalities that persisted within the Church of England's inherited pattern of rich and poor livings, and beneficed and unbeneficed clergy. The gulf between rich rector and poor curate was glaringly apparent. The parsonages that survive best are often the grandest. In poorer parishes existing parsonages might remain little improved, the responsibility for maintenance and refurbishment falling to the incumbent. Also the gentlemanly lifestyle increasingly expected of clergy households was expensive. The income of a single living might be inadequate to meet such demands, a reason advanced for the pluralism and consequent absenteeism with which the Georgian Church has been particularly associated.

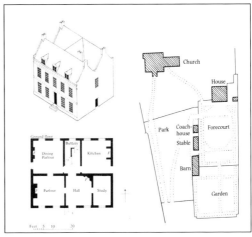

Suitable settings were important, as shown here at Wilford, Nottinghamshire, where the new rectory of c. 1720 was surrounded by a miniature park. (After M.W. Barley, 1986)

Where the parson held more than one living, parsonages might stand empty or be leased out or occupied by a cheaply paid curate. A clerical surplus provided a pool of unbeneficed ordained men who would stand in for their absent brethren. Carl Philip Moritz, a German visitor to England, observed the consequences of this. Walking from London to Oxford in June 1782, he stayed at an inn at Nettlebed in the Chilterns and decided to attend Sunday morning service. The local people put on their best clothes and the boys gathered at the entrance of the village to await the arrival of the priest, who came on horseback to take morning prayer at 9.30. Moritz followed the service in the Book of Common Prayer and heard a sturdy sermon in common language, but was most struck by the music of the west gallery choir and musicians. They sang Psalm 47. In the afternoon, with the priest gone, there was no divine service but the villagers made their own music, singing several psalms 'in so seemly a manner that it might have been a kind of service too'. As he walked on, Moritz fell into company with a clergyman, who turned out to be the Reverend Mr Modd, chaplain of Corpus Christi College, Oxford. He had taken service in Dorchester that afternoon. Conversing in Latin, they reached Oxford at midnight and Modd took Moritz to the Mitre Inn on the High Street, where they found 'a whole roomful of clergymen in their gowns and cravats sitting round a great table with their beer-mugs in front of them'. These were the jobbing parsons without parsonages, who gathered particularly in towns, preaching, teaching and doing duty as the opportunity arose.

Other clerical town dwellers escaped the tedium of rural residence. In 1832 nine parish incumbents and eleven curates from surrounding parishes were living in Louth, prompting Bishop Kaye of Lincoln to call it a 'nest of rooks'. By 1853 just one incumbent and one curate from 'outside' parishes lived there; a reforming divide had been crossed and non-residence had become unacceptable.

The Reverend William Cole (1714–82), diarist and rector of Bletchley, Buckinghamshire.

In the parsonages of Georgian England the wide-ranging roles of the parson, as seen in the sixteenth and seventeenth centuries, continued – civil, economic and secular as well as religious. The majority of parishes remained rural, but the traditional system they represented was faced from the mid-century with more people, modernising agriculture and landscapes, increased urban living, transformations in work and employment, commercial and industrial growth, and new debates about religion and politics. These brought questioning of church patronage, property,

Dissenting competition. The Baptist manse at Aston, near Bampton, Oxfordshire, the imposing house where the ministers of Cote Baptist chapel lived from c. 1740 to 1958. There was no Anglican church in Aston or Cote until 1839.

power, accountability and standards of provision. Inside views, which by the eighteenth century were increasingly available in letters and diaries, paint a vivid picture of parsonage life in this period, as in this diary entry by William Cole, rector of Bletchley, Buckinghamshire, for 10 December 1767:

> Rainy at Times, but fine Day. Masons making a Gutter & Sink in the Brewhouse. Mary Phillips cleaning the House after them. Married Wm Baxter to Mary Howell, 2 Methodists, with whom this Parish swarms. Levet hedging & ditching the Close. Unpacked several Boxes of China &c. Had a Teal for Dinner. Buried Mr Jacklyn at 5 o'clock.

Cole was a gentleman antiquary, bachelor and diarist, who saw the basic duties of his ministry done but was full of other concerns. He was a farming parson, going into the fields to see the haymaking and collecting his tithes. His patron, Browne Willis, lived at nearby Whaddon Hall, and Cole

William Cole's 1765 drawing of Bletchley parsonage, an ancient house that he began remodelling shortly after becoming rector in 1753.

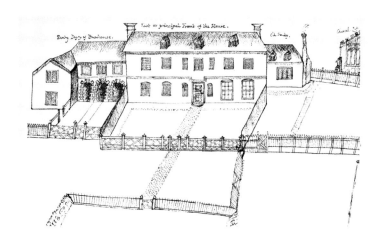

William Cole was keenly conscious of the latest cultural fashions. The grounds of his parsonage featured eclectic examples, including this elegant light and airy Chinese and Gothic temple and a hermitage (right).

paid close attention to him and his family, bringing gifts, for example from a visit to Paris. Cole's correspondents included Horace Walpole. There was a round of visiting and socialising, official duties including the turnpike trust, and customary involvements in the annual round of high days and holidays, often with associated charitable gifts to parishioners.

In all of this the parsonage next to the church was central. Soon after his arrival in 1753 Cole was rebuilding the rambling house in brick. It was in the remodelled rectory parlour that he found himself, on a cold January day in 1766, having just married a couple with children out of wedlock and brought them in to sign the register in the warmth, agreeing to baptise their infant and church the mother there. '[I]t was absurd to do it in a Parlour,' he tells his diary, yet if he refused parishioners these days 'they will either abstain from all Ordinances, or go over to the Dissenters'.

The hospitality of the parsonage continued, although in carefully graduated form. After Sunday service some parishioners dined with Cole, whilst the parish clerk and others

were catered for in the kitchen. Outside, the stables, coach-house, dovecote, wood and tithe barns and farmyard remained. There was now also a ha-ha, a sunken wall that protected Cole's boundaries but did not interrupt his views. His parsonage grounds also included a gravel terrace, grass walk, espalier fruit trees, hot beds, and beds for asparagus, scarlet strawberries, spinach, cucumbers, carrots, potatoes, broccoli, savoys, celery and more. The *pièce de résistance* comprised the 'elegant light and airy Chinese & Gothic Temple', hexagonal with matching table and chairs, where he delighted to sit with guests, and the Hermitage. Cole's minutely detailed description of every feature and furnishing of house and grounds and the views to and from them are eloquent testimony to the scale and significance of a mid-Georgian parsonage for the incumbent, his household and parishioners.

Cole altered a rambling existing house rather than build anew. We can also picture a purpose-built Georgian parsonage by using another inventory and parson's diary, those of John Longe, vicar of Coddenham, Suffolk, from 1797 to 1834. Reporting for the bishop's visitation of 1820, he wrote: 'There are no families of note … but that of the vicar.' The vicarage was the principal house of the parish and from it he strove to exercise leadership in the community, a cross between parson and squire. He was resident and held no other living. He preached and conducted regular services, meeting his own and many contemporary expectations, if exhibiting little spiritual zeal. Longe kept a household of ten servants (in 1835 the living was valued at £1,009 a year), farmed and socialised in Suffolk and Norfolk. He trained young curates, who were paid £100 a year and a house, was a magistrate, was Tory in politics, was involved with the turnpike trust and house of industry and was litigious in defending his tithe rights.

Longe's vicarage had been built in 1775 by the Bacon family, who owned the living. He came to Coddenham as curate in 1790 and within the year had married the

Coddenham Vicarage, in east Suffolk, built in 1775 to serve the living owned by the Bacon family. The grandest house in the parish, its occupant was a 'squarson', combining the roles of squire and parson. (From a watercolour by an unknown artist, now in private hands)

sister-in-law of the incumbent, Nicholas Bacon. When Bacon died in 1797, Longe was appointed to this plum family living. It seems to have been then that he compiled an inventory of the rooms and contents (although not the servants' quarters) of the parsonage. There was an entrance vestibule, staircase and upper vestibule, library, common parlour, great dining parlour with bow window, drawing room, housekeeper's room and three bedchambers and a dressing room. Their contents speak of contemporary consumerism – furniture, painted floor cloths, Wilton carpets, Manchester green and white upholstery fabrics, India fire screens, and Worcester china. The paintings on display ranged from biblical scenes to royalty, patriotic events such as the Spanish Armada and family portraits. There was a Wedgwood bust of Lord Bacon, a camera obscura and Dr Priestley's apparatus for making mineral water. Longe's bedchamber was decorated with red and white check wallpaper, red furniture and a red carpet. In it he kept seven guns: blunderbusses, horse and pocket pistols.

In the stables was a post-chaise and in the cellars sherry, port, Madeira, gin, hock, brandy, rum, cider and cowslip wine.

At Coddenham we see a grand, modern and prosperously endowed Georgian parsonage. Perhaps more typical of a medium-sized living was the rectory at Weston Longville, some 8 miles from Norwich, where from 1776 to his death in 1803 perhaps the best-known of all clerical diarists, James Woodforde, was parson. It has been calculated that a rural Georgian clergyman could keep open house, with four to five servants, on around £400 a year. This is what Woodforde, a bachelor, did.

In 1779 Woodforde's eighteen-year-old niece, Nancy, came to keep house for him and remained for twenty-four years. She was one of eight children of a clerical family, part of the more modest reaches of the dense network of ecclesiastical and family connections and interests that permeate the period. Her own diary for 1792 provides a woman's-eye view of parsonage life. She received a yearly allowance from her uncle, a £10 banknote for clothes and pocket money. Her life was constrained by gentility and geography. She mixed with only a few suitable neighbours and despaired when the kindly local squires, the Custances, moved away to Bath. There is a strong sense of rural isolation, with travel not possible from November until spring. The rectory garden was a godsend; there Nancy could walk alone, recording as much as 4 miles a day, if weather allowed. Her other main occupations were sewing, reading and occasionally singing, playing cribbage for money with her uncle and reading him sermons on Sunday evenings. In March 1792 she wrote, 'Not a soul has call'd on us this week. No letters from our friends.

Nancy Woodforde, drawn by her brother, Samuel. Niece and housekeeper of a famous clerical diarist, James Woodforde, rector of Weston Longville, near Norwich, Nancy's own diary provides a woman's-eye view of parsonage life in 1792.

We spend our time reading.' The year's monotony was relieved by three trips to Norwich, with shopping, the hairdressers, theatre and a concert. There is none of the busy and energising round of local welfare, charity or educational parish work so familiar amongst the women folk of later parsonages.

Servants were an essential feature of Georgian parsonages. Woodforde and Cole both had five (men and women and a boy), sufficient to put them on a level with comfortably off lay neighbours. Recruitment was local, by personal knowledge and recommendation, sometimes helping needy children or a relative of an existing servant – another miniature world of patronage. Servants trained in a clergyman's house were well-regarded and could be put in the way of good jobs elsewhere. The parsonage also generated considerable part-time work, in farming, gardening and housework, from cooking, to laundry, to cleaning, to special entertaining. After haymaking at Bletchley, Cole had thirty workers to supper in the parsonage kitchen. Sometimes servants were a problem – skiving, drunk, noisy, saucy, disrespectful, or illegitimately pregnant. But many stayed for years as loyal supporters and, given the sometimes isolated nature of parsonage life, important company and contact for the clergy family.

How did the parsonage appear to parishioners? A telling contemporary perspective is provided by Thomas Turner, the village shopkeeper of East Hoathly, East Sussex. His diary dates from 1754 to 1765, when, in his twenties and thirties, he was also at times scribe, teacher, surveyor, undertaker, churchwarden and parish overseer. This brought Turner into constant contact with the rector, Thomas Porter, to whose house he delivered goods from his shop, in whose church he regularly worshipped, and with whom he discussed parish rates and poor law cases and beat the parish bounds. These many official involvements made Turner part of the parish elite, but always at a remove in status from 'Mr Porter'. All the more shocking, then, that during a hectic winter round

of parties in early 1758 Turner and his wife found themselves at the parsonage and other elite houses for a series of all-night sessions of eating, drinking, gambling on cards and dancing. Finally, on 22 February, the 'downright obstreperous mirth mixed with a great deal of folly and stupidity' became too much for Turner. He left early, at 3.30 a.m., only to be awakened at 6 a.m. by the Porters and other revellers who dragged Turner from his bed and made him dance in his wife's petticoat. 'The drunken perambulation' continued until 3.30 p.m. Turner was left with a severe hangover and, although unshaken in his loyalty to Church and Crown (the two inextricable in his mind), reflecting that 'precepts delivered from the pulpit by Mr Porter … must lose a great deal of their efficacy by such examples'. Such clerical behaviour he would always think 'contrary as well to the Christian religion as to my own conscience'. There were clearly lines between parson and flock that should not be crossed from either side.

The Georgian parsonage may seem to epitomise a national church that has been much criticised, whether by contemporary political opponents, by nineteenth-century

The dark stones of Haworth Parsonage, Yorkshire (1778–9) provided a fitting home for the Brontë sisters, whose father, Patrick, resided here as vicar from 1820–61. The newer wing to the right was added by his successor, Reverend John Wade.

clerical reformers or by later historians. Some recent historians have been kinder in their judgements, pointing to clergy who were conscientious and caring in the context of the period rather than worldly, unenthusiastic and neglectful, and stressing active eighteenth-century debates on faith, belief, theology and practice. The story behind Joseph Wright of Derby's fine 1786 portrait of the Reverend Thomas Gisborne and his wife Mary points up this ambivalence. Thomas on the face of it seems to sum up much that was questionable about the Georgian Establishment. He had inherited Yoxhall Lodge, near Derby, and a sizeable income, having attended Harrow and Cambridge. However, instead of becoming an MP, he followed his vocation and was ordained in 1783. He was presented to a local family living, which he held in plurality, being also a prebendary of Durham Cathedral. He dabbled in the natural history of the surrounding Needwood Forest. But Thomas may also represent the conscientious and high-minded clergyman of the period. He, Mary and their eight children lived a settled life in the main family house, which now also became a parsonage. His ministry was influenced by the Evangelical Revival that from the 1730s had become an increasingly strong force in English religion, both within the Church of England and outside it, particularly seen in the rise of Methodism. This strong individual and biblical faith, allied to active and practical good works in daily life, was reflected in Thomas Gisborne's local ministry, in his restrained dress, in his writings on such topics as the duties of men in the higher ranks and middle classes, and in his association with the Clapham Sect. This group demonstrated the leading role of Evangelical thinking in Anglicanism in the late eighteenth and early nineteenth centuries. It included Gisborne's old university friend, William Wilberforce, who visited the Gisbornes at Yoxhall and whose belief that slavery must be abolished Thomas shared. This was a parson who was a product of the old regime, yet prefigures the onset of change.

Whatever the motivation of clergy to live in their parishes or chapelries and minister directly to their parishioners, the harsh fact remained that the Church's resources were so unevenly distributed that consistent provision, including an adequate house for a resident parson, was not possible. This was a state church that was not government-funded but dependent on a maze of inherited, locally varying endowments, some now in lay hands. The first government interventions aimed at tackling these problems of parsonage provision occurred during the early eighteenth century. Queen Anne's Bounty was established in 1704 'for the augmentation of the maintenance of poor clergy'. Initial investigations showed that 5,082 livings fell below its threshold of income of at least £80 a year. In 1715 the Bounty's remit was extended to include curacies and chapelries, where some of the poorest livings were concentrated. The first grants to augment livings were made in 1714; by 1800 over five thousand capital grants had been made, increasing the Church's endowments by some £1.5 million. Between 1801 and 1840 further Bounty grants totalled some £2 million. The money was to be used to buy local land to create a permanent source of income. In 1777 Gilbert's Act provided for the mortgaging of livings to allow Queen Anne's Bounty to make loans for the building or repair of parsonages. By 1826 over five hundred loans had been made. The pressure to ensure residence grew, with legislation in 1803 requiring bishops to make annual returns of non-resident clergy. An 1817

The Reverend Thomas Gisborne and his wife Mary, in a portrait dated 1786 by Joseph Wright of Derby.

Traditional responses to changing times? The imposing, late-Georgian parsonage of a new parish at Falstone, Northumberland, created in 1811.

return to Parliament of clerical residences showed over two thousand benefices with unfit residences and 2,600 with no parsonage at all. Progress had been made, the income of poor livings had been increased and some parsonages built or repaired, but the problem remained formidable. The response was still to tinker with individual livings within a wildly varying network and, where new churches were needed, to create and individually endow new parish areas on the historic parish pattern. These were expected to have substantial parsonages, as seen at Falstone, Northumberland, a new parish of 250 square miles and two townships, taken out of the huge ancient parish of Sandiburn in 1811. Its imposing late Georgian clergy house stands in bleak isolation.

Such efforts were signs that the Church was not readily able to cope with maintaining its material and spiritual fabric, nor with changing to meet the new demands that were gathering pace. The constitutional revolution of 1828 to 1832 affected the Church greatly. Its institutional monopoly was lost in 1828 and 1829, as first Protestant Nonconformists and then Roman Catholics were given full political rights. Then there was turmoil over parliamentary reform, a battle in which twenty-one of twenty-seven Anglican bishops voted in the Lords against the Reform Bill. The Church of England was deeply implicated in the old order. The parsonage was an uncomfortable place to be. At a time of peak unrest in the Anglican rural heartlands the clergy were confronted by demands to reduce tithes and to relieve distress by raising wages, preventing loss of work through the introduction of machinery, and ensuring humane Poor Law policies. They were the local representatives of authority and in the front line of confrontation. In Norfolk the incumbent of Edingthorpe reported 'a mob at the kitchen door' in July 1831. Thirty other Norfolk clergy had similar experiences. During the Swing Riots of 1830 the High Sheriff of Kent was told that 'we will destroy the corn-stacks and threshing machines this year. Next year we will have a turn with the parsons, and the third we will make war upon the statesmen.' At St Mary Bourne, Hampshire, the parson was accused of preaching 'against the poor'. When Samuel Wilberforce, son of William and himself a future reforming Victorian bishop, took up his first living at Checkendon in the Chilterns in 1828, he and his young wife, Emily, felt this threatening climate keenly. Samuel was advised by the outgoing parson to ensure a live-in manservant, who would not only cut the wood and draw the water but 'sleep downstairs with a gun loaded with ball at his side and a sword-stick'. Emily Wilberforce received letters from her sister in their father's rectory at Lavington in Sussex telling of men coming to the kitchen door. 'Howick the shoemaker … carried a lanthorn which Papa has no doubt was a sign that he meant to burn the stacks if he did not get what he wanted … The barn is still watched every night, and will be so till it is insured.' Challenging times indeed, and clergy such as Samuel Wilberforce, who had experienced them, would go on to lead the Church into a period of immense reinvigoration in which parsonages were to boom in numbers and significance.

Parsonages became a focus for increasing protest in the early nineteenth century. In this cover illustration of *The Life and History of Swing, the Kent Rick Burner*, published in 1830, a portly parson on horseback encounters a family in dire distress. In the background burning hayricks, a church and grand house can be seen.

VICTORIAN AND EDWARDIAN HEYDAY

Fʀᴏᴍ ᴛʜᴇ 1830s the Church poured vast effort into building unprecedented numbers of new or enhanced parsonages, as it sought to reform itself whilst simultaneously facing increased external pressure to change. The parsonage became a key part of a very traditional response through local parochial ministry to new, modern and pressing challenges. It was essential to realising the Church's ideal of a resident clergyman in every parish, a man who could devote his whole time and energy to his ministry, and preferably was married with a family to act as a pattern and a monitor for the community.

Just how pressing was the need to change was revealed when the results of the unique national census of religious provision and attendance, taken in 1851, were published. They showed that Protestant Dissenters had nearly half the sittings in places of worship in England and Wales. Dissenters also accounted for over 40 per cent of Sunday morning worshippers and two-thirds of those in the evening. Nor was it just a matter of competing for shares of an observant population. The statistics also showed that of some 12.5 million potential worshippers on Census Sunday, almost 5.3 million had not attended worship. These were shocking headlines for Anglicans, further galvanising processes of reform that were already well underway. They were defending their role as the national church at a time when governmental changes were dismantling many of Anglicanism's old monopolies and roles. Moreover, this was happening when the people they were seeking to retain or win

All Saints, Margaret Street, London – a new urban church and parsonage, completed in 1853 and designed by a leading architect, William Butterfield. (From *The Builder*, 1853)

The Victorian ideal of a clerical family in a suitably substantial parsonage, personified by the Reverend Thomas Evetts and his family at Monks Risborough, Buckinghamshire, in an undated photo (probably from the 1860s).

were rapidly rising in numbers, with many living different lives and often in very different places from those which the Church of England's traditional parish infrastructure had been intended to reach.

The mid-century was a time of rationalisation of existing organisation at diocesan, cathedral and parish level, of the creation of new benefices, of attempted redistribution and equalisation of endowments, of increased clergy residence in parishes, of the eradication of pluralism, of church building and restoration, of more frequent worship and changing liturgy, of shifts in the pastoral and secular roles of local clergy, and (enabling much of this) improved clergy housing. During the nineteenth century 3,760 new parishes or 'ecclesiastical districts' were created, and with them new parsonages. Provision for industrialising, urbanising or suburbanising areas was particularly urgent. In the area of the new (1847) diocese of Manchester 415 Church of England churches were built between 1800 and 1914, whilst in the ancient parish of Manchester 136 new parishes had been created by 1914.

When it came to motive, resources and action to build local parsonages, it was often individuals and families, clergy and lay, who got the work done. Bishops and archdeacons might press, investigate and encourage but they were dependent on those on the ground to act, and to find most or all of the money needed. Support for parsonage building was widespread, but one group within the Church was newly influential. The High Church Oxford Movement had begun in 1833, in defence of the Church of England as the true national church against encroaching government interference and a perceived rejection of faith in English society. For

Tractarians (as the early adherents of the movement were known, from the *Tracts for the Times*, through which they disseminated their views between 1833 and 1841), the rediscovery of faith and of the Church's role was to be rooted in a return to a supposed historic pattern of parish life. In this the local priest led a community united by Christian values not only in worship but in every aspect of their lives, from education to welfare. This reassertion of the priestly role, enforced at ordination by the authority of apostolic succession, gave the home of the priest a central importance, practically, spiritually and aesthetically. As Tractarian influence spread to parish level, so their enthusiasm for medievalism was reflected in the architectural style of many Victorian clergy houses. The parsonage, with the church and the church school, was typically part of a triumvirate of influential local buildings. Parsonage design attracted some of the best contemporary architects and led the way in the development of small and medium house styles for gentlemanly Victorians.

Kidmore End, near Reading, a new parish of 1854. It was one of many created as the Church of England strove to respond to change. The parish magazine cover of 1861 sums up the practical priorities: a new parsonage, a new church and a modern water supply.

Pugin, Butterfield, Street, Gilbert Scott, Pearson and Bodley all designed parsonages, as did many other architects of varying national or local reputation. Two clergy houses, both designed in 1845, became highly influential examples of the quintessential Victorian parsonage. At Rampisham, Dorset, A. W. N. Pugin was commissioned by Frederick Rooke, a young incumbent influenced by Tractarianism at Oxford, to design a new parsonage (see page 4). Built between 1845 and 1847, Rampisham rectory has been described by Pugin's biographer, Rosemary Hill, as 'perfectly poised between revival and invention'. It sets aside polite classicism and symmetry, with rubble stone walls, each face different, a gable breaking forward to create light and shade, the whole set amid a garden. It evokes tradition and Englishness, but is not a slavish pastiche of vernacular buildings. At Coalpit Heath, a former mining area near Bristol that was 'proverbial for vice and irreligion', William Butterfield (also in 1845) was designing a parsonage, described by *The Buildings of England* as 'a seminal building, archetype of hundreds of Victorian parsonages'. The vicarage follows Butterfield's principle that the exterior should reflect the needs of internal planning, not vice versa. The result is a building which is asymmetrical, with a variety of windows, tracery and mouldings, its form broken by gables and chimney breast, aware of stylistic precedents, related to local traditional building and to Gothic features, but not tied to any one previous style.

The parsonage became a generalised building type. Its essentials were identified by Robert Kerr in his *The Gentleman's House, or How to Plan English Residences from the Parsonage to the Palace* (second edition, 1865). The clergy house exemplified the modest end of a spectrum of shared sensibility and practical design recognised throughout Britain as appropriate to 'the domestic habits of refined persons'. The essential qualities were quiet comfort for his family and guests; thorough convenience for his domestics; and elegance and importance without ostentation.

A key element for Kerr was the separation of the family from servants; 'what passes on either side of the boundary shall be both invisible and inaudible to the other.' Kerr chose Fillongley Vicarage in Warwickshire (1859) to represent a small house of such a kind. He approved its south-facing drawing- and dining-rooms

The vicarage at Coalpit Heath, near Bristol, designed by William Butterfield in 1845 and described as the 'archetype of hundreds of Victorian parsonages'.

GROUND FLOOR   FIRST FLOOR

The ideal Victorian vicarage, with its carefully segregated plan, represented by Fillongley, Warwickshire (1859). Fillongley was chosen by Robert Kerr to exemplify the best in parsonage design in his book *The Gentleman's House*.

of equal size as the principal family rooms. The dining-room has a hatch to the butler's pantry but definitely no direct link to the kitchen, which should be as well shut off as possible. A separate side entrance allows access to the vicar's study and to the servants' zone without disturbing the family. A back stair proves possible even in a small house and allows the separation of family and servants. However, Kerr felt one WC inadequate for a house of this size.

Kerr's criteria and design rules can be seen applied in many local parsonages, sometimes in surviving buildings and also in the deposited plans for proposed parsonages that accompanied applications for funding to Queen Anne's Bounty or to the growing number of diocesan societies, established to support church and parsonage building or restoration. (The first, in Exeter diocese, was formed in 1841.) G. E. Street, the eminent diocesan architect of Oxford, commenting in 1853 on a parsonage plan, criticised the strength of timbers, the size of upper windows, ceiling heights of less than 9 feet 6 inches and the location of a WC immediately facing the drawing-room. Kerr would have approved, although his butler's pantry might have been realised less often. A study of household servants in seventy Norfolk parishes in 1851 and 1901 shows an average

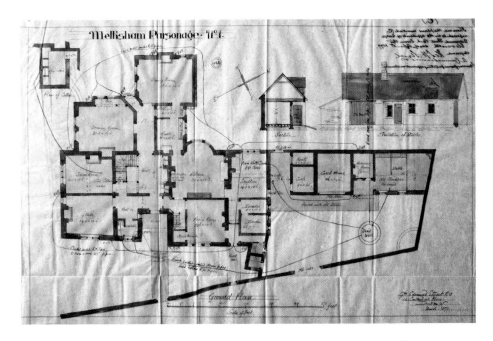

Many plans of new or remodelled parsonages survive in central church or local diocesan archives. At Melksham, Wiltshire, in 1877, G. E. Street was the architect for this adaptation, with the old vicarage absorbed into the kitchen as extensive additions (shown in red) were made.

of 2.5 and 2.3 per household, typically with all female living-in servants and no butlers or footmen. Plans for 619 new or extended parsonages between 1791 and 1906 survive in Norwich diocesan records. The peaks of building were in the periods 1840–9 (84), 1860–9 (85) and 1870–9 (80).

Parsonage building was significantly influenced by increasing outside intervention in church life. Government investigation and legislation gathered pace after 1830. The Royal Commission on Ecclesiastical Revenues was set up in 1831 to enquire into the distribution of income within the Church as a preliminary to necessary changes. Information was collected on bishoprics, cathedrals and collegiate churches and from 10,540 local incumbents. The Commission's first two reports were followed by transfer of some income from bishoprics and deans and chapters to central funds to support new sees, new livings and to augment poor livings. Its third report in 1835 provided the most reliable record since the 1535 *Valor Ecclesiasticus* of the location and income of local livings. It still showed great inequalities of income and provision. An initial target was set, to provide a minister for each population of two thousand and over and with an annual stipend of at least £150. A third of livings reported in 1835 fell below this £150 threshold, with the highest numbers in the dioceses of York, Chester and Lincoln. This was in a range of livings where annual incomes of £150–£249 have been accounted respectable, £250–£349 comfortable, and £350 and above wealthy. The Church was urged to encourage private benefactions to endow livings and to transfer patronage in lay hands to bishops.

In 1836 the Ecclesiastical Commission was made permanent, with a membership of bishops and politicians. It managed the central funds accruing from the surplus assets of bishoprics, deans and chapters and directed them to augmenting poor and populous livings, to establishing new district churches, and to building and improving parsonages. It also ensured legislative reforms. The Pluralities Act of 1838, drafted by the Commission, severely restricted the circumstances in which a clergyman could hold more than one living and limited the bishops' powers to license pluralism. Many pluralist clergy felt obliged to resign livings, and new appointments were made then or when an incumbent moved or died. The Parsonages Act of 1838 allowed bishops to require the building or repair of parsonages in livings worth more than £100 per year. The message was clear, and the 1840s saw abrupt falls in non-residence and a boom in parsonage building, a process which could put severe financial pressure on incumbents now obliged to respond to the requirements of a more centralised, proactive and bureaucratic state and church.

Other national changes were profoundly affecting local parsons. The Tithe Commutation Act of 1836 finally tackled the contentious exaction that was central to the income of many clergy. A central Tithe Commission was established in London, its secretariat and assistant commissioners charged with surveying and valuing land and property in 12,275 tithe districts (most often parishes). The surveys were the basis for attributing a rent-charge in lieu of tithes to individual properties. These charges would vary according to a septennial average of national corn prices. By 1852, 11,395 tithe districts were covered by tithe apportionments. In some other parishes tithe had already been rationalised as part of pre-1836 parliamentary enclosures. In such cases the parson was typically allocated enclosed land in lieu of tithes. Some clergy thus became owners of additional land. Others received a more predictable income through commutation and rent-charges. Either way they were relieved of the worldly and often argumentative process of collecting tithes in circumstances that varied according to the crop, the parishioner and local custom. The rationalisation was mostly welcome. It would be less so with the onset of prolonged agricultural depression from the mid-1870s. This meant that rural clergy in particular saw significant falls in income as the corn prices, to which tithe rent-charges were tied, declined.

It was also during the remarkable growth of government in the 1830s that the system of parish government, which

A gathering of Victorian clergy at Mentmore, Buckinghamshire. From the 1830s the clergy grew in numbers, were resident in their parishes and became increasingly professionalised.

Making the parsonage the focus of local life – maypole dancing on the lawn of the local vicarage (built in 1856) at Dorchester-on-Thames, Oxfordshire.

had given parish clergy such significant roles and status, was dismantled in favour of secular, state-led provision. Most notably, the Poor Law Amendment Act of 1834 ended poor relief delivered directly by the parish, replacing it with Poor Law unions, workhouses, and another government department, designed to determine every detail of policy and practice centrally. In 1837 civil registration replaced the national role of parish registers.

Other changes to parsonage life had more to do with a shift of culture and expectations, which has been called a 'professionalisation' of the clergy. The number of clerical magistrates declined in the face of criticism that to sit in criminal judgement on their flock was at odds with pastoral priorities and parochial harmony. The sporting, hunting cleric was increasingly frowned on, respectable restraint and unostentatious example to all classes becoming the expected tone. There was a growth in time spent in local schools, in visiting and all manner of charity, welfare and leisure provision which brought the parson or his family into contact with his flock outside church.

However, it remained hard to tell incumbents with parson's freehold what to do. This was particularly apparent in livings

The independent incumbent. Not all clergy conformed to new Victorian expectations. The Reverend John ('Jack') Russell was perpetual curate of Swimbridge, Devon, from 1831 to 1880, and resisted all his bishop's efforts to stop him hunting.

where established patronage or financial rights made for independence and resistance to change. In new, less well-endowed livings, more likely to be in church patronage from the start, the clergyman's position and outlook might be more open to 'new' ways, whether from necessity, deference or conviction. As opportunities for handsome incomes acquired through pluralism disappeared, so the number of graduates seeking ordination declined, as was obvious by about 1860. More non-graduates were being ordained. Some measure of clerical training developed, although only after the First World War was a year's training in a theological college required of graduates before ordination. It remained the case that Victorian clergy, like their parsonages, were expected above all to be gentlemanly. This 'gentleman heresy' was famously identified in the 1830s by Hurrell Froude, an early leader of the Oxford Movement. He considered that 'The kind of evangelism necessary for an urban, industrialised society could not be encompassed by a Church which was based on privilege and class'.

Anthony Trollope's Barsetshire novels offer us a spectrum of parsons and parsonages in this period of transition for the Church. They range from the comfortable splendours of Archdeacon Grantly, supported by private income and patronage at Plumsted Episcopi , to the unimproved vernacular vicarages and poor clergy of Puddingdale and Hogglestock, to the painful controversies surrounding the enforced reform of the historic foundation of Hiram's Hospital, with all the while a fictionalised version of *The Times* thundering censoriously. In reality more and more clergy were required to minister in urban and industrial places of quite a different kind. It is a contrast described by Trollope in *The Vicar of*

Bullhampton (1870). The eponymous Reverend Frank Fenwick is young and handsome and was at Oxford with his friend, the squire. Fenwick is married to an heiress, who is:

> as good a specimen of an English country parson's wife as you shall meet ... gay, good-looking, fond of the society around her ... knowing in blankets and corduroys and coals and tea ... acquainted with every man and woman in the parish; thinking her husband to be quite as good as the squire in regard to position ... a handsome, pleasant, well-dressed lady, who has no nonsense about her.

The Fenwicks live in a well-appointed vicarage, with a trout stream at the bottom of the garden. Loring is an industrial town, not far distant geographically but very distant in every other sense. Its genteel residents live in Loring Uphill. Loring Lowtown is:

> vulgar, dirty, devoted to commercial and manufacturing purposes ... [T]he parsonage ... stood apart from its neighbours, inside great tall slate-coloured gates, and ... had a garden of its own. But except for the clergyman,

Vicarage comforts – the sitting-room at Turkdean Vicarage, Gloucestershire, built in 1847 and photographed by Henry Taunt in 1900.

who had no choice in the matter, nobody who was anybody lived at Lowtown.

Victorian urban parsonages also drew the attention of leading architects. All Saints, Margaret Street, London, was designed in 1849 by William Butterfield and completed in 1853 (page 60). It is a model church of those arbiters of Gothic Revival building the Ecclesiological Society (founded in 1839 as the Cambridge Camden Society and renamed in 1845). The church embodies High Church principles of sacramental worship, and uses brick to decorate the construction in innovative ways. Its interest for the student of urban parsonages lies in the combination on a city site little more than 100 feet square of a church, choir school, dining room, classrooms and clergy house for the vicar, two curates and servants.

Newly developed urban areas allowed more space. In 1840 the Great Western Railway (GWR) chose a green-field site at Swindon for their locomotive works. Soon the engineering shed and, by 1842, workers' terraced housing, had sprung up. One of the first actions was to create a new ecclesiastical parish, St Mark's. First came the parsonage and school and house, then the church, consecrated in 1845. The cost of the three buildings, £8,386, was met by public subscription and the GWR, who also paid the stipend of the perpetual curate. The company gave no support to non-Anglicans. St Mark's vicarage of 1844 had an entrance hall, dining- and drawing-rooms, study and four bedrooms. In 1888 a stable yard and service wing were added. It was, in appearance and concept, very like its rural counterparts.

A plan of All Saints, Margaret Street, London, built between 1849 and 1853. A cramped urban site was used to great effect to bring together church, parish meeting place and vicarage (in the block to the right of the courtyard).

Edward Snell's 1849 panorama of Swindon, with the new railway town still taking shape. On the left are the engineering works and main railway line with, in the foreground, the Anglican church of St Mark's. Its parsonage and school (with maypole dancing in the yard) are next to terraced workers' housing.

Although adapted according to particular urban sites, the similarity in aspiration of urban and rural parsonages persisted, as indicated by two examples of the late 1860s. The iron-making town of Middlesbrough saw some of the most rapid mid-century growth of any English town. The parsonage of St John the Evangelist, built between 1864 and 1866 by John Norton, shows ambitious scale, and the diffusion of High Victorian brick patterning and polychromy, although now with less 'correct' Gothic detailing.

St Mark's Vicarage, Swindon, Wiltshire, built in 1844 and extended in 1888.

The vicarage of St Barnabas, Jericho, Oxford, was built to serve a new parish (1869) in a still-developing working-class suburb. Modest in scale, but double-fronted amongst the surrounding terraces, it is still in use. Here, the first vicar is reputed to have extracted the teeth of parishioners who could not afford other treatment.

An altogether grander Victorian suburban vicarage is G. E. Street's design of 1854 at Boyn Hill, Maidenhead, in Berkshire, where All Saints was built in anticipation of the respectable villa expansion of the town. Another Tractarian-influenced building, it is grouped with a school, schoolmaster's house, further clergy house and nearby almshouse.

Funds for urban church and parsonage building and maintenance were not always easy to find. At Boyn Hill the money came from lay benefactors. Other possible sources included grants from Queen Anne's Bounty, the Ecclesiastical Commission or diocesan societies. Otherwise subscriptions, fundraising and the incumbent's own income were the main options. In urban and industrial areas clerical incomes were often low, and incumbents less likely to have private means. Nor were prominent local laity guaranteed to support the local Anglican parish. Indeed, they might be active in other denominations. Mark Smith has suggested that in Oldham and Saddleworth in the 1830s 'clergymen without private means or additional employment were not too far removed from the position of skilled cotton workers'.

When Thomas Lowe of St Mary's, Oldham, applied to the Ecclesiastical Commissioners for a grant to build a parsonage they required a larger design, which was beyond his means. Only in 1865, twenty-one years after Lowe's first attempt, was a parsonage built. Another local

The vicarage of St Barnabas, Jericho, Oxford, newly built in 1869, sits beside the canal and remains the parsonage of this Anglo-Catholic urban parish.

minister wrote to the Commissioners in 1856 of the difficulties of working in such an area: 'It took me two years to get up my church and five or six more to clear it of debt, during which time I wrote in my own hand from one to two thousand letters soliciting contributions in all parts of the country.' He had then raised over £1,000 to erect schools. He could not keep going back to the same sources and, in any case, felt it wrong to beg for support for a parsonage, as opposed to church or schools. 'Such a course by lowering the clerical character, would tend to impede one's usefulness, to say nothing of personal feeling.'

Boyn Hill, Maidenhead, Berkshire, a suburban religious complex designed by G. E. Street in 1854, and pictured in *The Builder* in 1860. The vicarage lies to the right of the church.

The need to beg and borrow might compromise the clergyman's role as pastor. It also put individual clergy into debt. This applied also to the maintenance of parsonages. Outgoing clergy were expected to leave these in good repair or to pay a sum to cover repair of dilapidations. The Ecclesiastical Dilapidations Act of 1871, providing for inspections by archdeacons of vacant benefice buildings and for the Queen Anne's Bounty fund to oversee the necessary works, was another centralised solution to a difficult process.

Victorian parsonages represent an enormous investment of resources, effort and faith. They symbolise the Church's answer to how it might remain as the national established church with a ministry extended to all in a much-changed society. Did parsonages succeed? In late Victorian and Edwardian England organised religion remained ubiquitous in most people's lives, from birth to death. Rites of passage were widely observed in religious form. Churches remained leading providers of education. Their role in delivering charity and welfare provision was significant. Much of the vocabulary of respectable public mores was religious. The Church of England was still

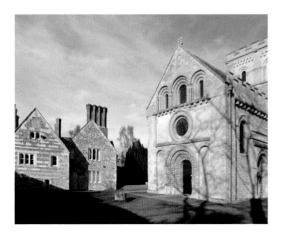

Making ends meet; tutoring and schoolmastering were ways for clergy to earn extra income. The Old Parsonage, Iffley, Oxfordshire, in 1851 contained two clerical households; one was headed by the 27-year-old Reverend William Slatter and his mother, and contained twenty-one boy boarders aged eight to fourteen.

established, and much involved in national and civic rituals. Yet there were now many large and confident alternative religious denominations, and a significant amount of non-observance, indifference or rejection. Other ways to organise those things for which the parson might have been the natural intermediary – welfare, charity or education – were developing through central and local government and collective and individual effort. Amidst this altered landscape the parsonage stood, representing a traditional hierarchy and authority to which people were expected to turn. Parsonages were difficult to afford, and became more so. Clerical incomes remained variable, and many fell in real value from the 1870s. Although larger numbers of clergy were ordained, reaching 23,363 in England and Wales in 1901, the rise in overall population had been so rapid that it outpaced that growth. The ratio of clergy to population was rising again and continued to do so as the clergy numbers of 1901 proved to be a peak.

Differing perceptions of the Victorian parson and his parsonage are offered by Richard Jefferies, in *Hodge and His Masters* (1880), a mix of fictional and factual reflection. The clergyman sits in his parsonage garden, asleep in the shade, watched by his wife, who is tending beehives to raise a little money, for they are 'extremely poor', despite the spacious house and immaculately kept gardens. Her husband looks worn and older than he really is. He came to the parish as a young man, determined to do good by an undogmatic and practical Christianity of brotherhood and goodwill, involving himself in village life at every turn, but she now feels he is pushed aside. Some show resentment of his 'interference'.

Changing architectural styles are exemplified by Cefn Bryntalch, near Welshpool, a late Victorian design by G. F. Bodley, who moved from Gothic to Queen Anne style.

Others are openly hostile to the perceived riches and influence of the Church. In reality the parsonage roof is leaking and they are hard put to repair it. As she ponders in the garden, where 'there was an air of refinement everywhere', Hodge the farm labourer goes by atop a laden wagon and, looking over the hedge, 'thought to himself what a jolly life that parson led, sleeping away the hot hours in the shade'. The Victorian parsonage was meant to signal the presence and commitment of the Church in every locality, a place of support and leadership. Its gentlemanly buildings also set the clergy apart, as they strove in largely traditional ways to maintain their role in inescapably modern settings.

The Primitive Methodist chapel and chapel house at Yoxford, Suffolk, built 1856. Non-Anglican congregations were increasingly significant in many localities.

VICARAGES AND RECTORIES: THE RECENT PAST

IN THE TWENTIETH century the legacy of the Victorian boom in parsonage building passed to succeeding local clergy. Bishop Goodwin of Carlisle had anticipated this. Between 1860 and 1890 he saw 157 parsonages in his diocese built, rebuilt or improved. He reflected:

> Much as one delights in the thought of the clergy being housed in a manner befitting their habits and their recognised social position, I cannot but feel that in some cases a large house, built in an ornamental style, may become a heavy burden upon a slender income. I would wish that in not a few instances the purse of the incumbent, rather than the glory of the architect, had been manifestly the first consideration.

At Tewkesbury the spacious and updated former abbot's house was purchased in 1883 for the use of the then and future vicars. By 1919, the incoming incumbent announced in the parish magazine that he expected to be the last vicar to live there. 'Thank God the days are over when the parson was necessarily a man of large means.' Some might regret that vicars would be unable to keep up so big a house and garden, 'but can one possibly be sorry that the "parson" of the town should henceforth be more obviously on the same level as his parishioners'.

A substantial parsonage in every parish, so recently seen as key part of the Church's response to a changing society, was now often seen as a problem rather than a solution. Financial concerns, declining church attendances, the inflexible locations of historic churches and parsonages, the exclusive impression perhaps created by grand houses, a fall in clergy numbers all contributed to increasing debates over 'unsuitable parsonages'. In 1933 a clergy wife told the Church Assembly that 'a brass band playing in the kitchen would not be heard in any one of the other twenty-one rooms of her rural rectory'.

The Church Commissioners, formed in 1948 in succession to Queen Anne's Bounty and the Ecclesiastical Commission, are now responsible for acquiring and selling clergy houses and guiding the ideal design of the modern parsonage.

By 1930 nearly six hundred parsonages had already been sold, followed by another seven hundred by 1939. Some six hundred more 'suitable' replacements were built or purchased. After the Second World War the pace of sales increased. In 1948 the Ecclesiastical Commission and Queen Anne's Bounty were amalgamated to form the Church Commissioners. In the following fifty years over eight thousand parsonages were sold by the Church. Reduced maintenance and running costs, together with modern amenities for clergy and their families, were now primary considerations. In 1953 the Church Commissioners published their first *Parsonage Design Guide* with its specific guidelines on how to translate these requirements into built form. The guide's sixth edition established the benchmark for purpose-built parsonage design at the turn of the millennium. The parsonage should combine a home for the incumbent and his or (with the ordination of women from 1994) her family and a base in the local community for the parson's ministry. The house should provide public and private spaces, be welcoming but also ensure a necessary degree of security. With a total floor area of some 2,000 square feet, it should have an entrance lobby and study (200 square feet) for the parson, two family rooms and kitchen and a living room large enough for hospitality for parishioners, four bedrooms and garage. It should not look too different from surrounding properties.

Another criterion for the modern parsonage is that it should be saleable if local ministry needs to change. This reflects altered thinking and ongoing shifts in the historic framework of parishes and benefices that had determined the pattern of parsonages for so long. One approach has been to unite benefices, bringing together parishes with a beneficed incumbent, supported in his or her ministry by other clergy and laity, with increasing numbers of non-stipendiary clergy providing 'ordained local ministry'. In some areas pastoral schemes have created formal team ministries, headed by a team rector, holding the property of the former parishes. The rector will share the cure of souls with other full-time, stipendiary clergy, called team vicars. 'House for Duty' is a third option, where a priest lives in the parsonage without stipend and in return for providing local ministry. Retired priests or those working part-time in other roles may fulfil this role, as around four hundred clergy did in 2010. In these

St James's Vicarage, Oldham, Greater Manchester – a 1990s parsonage in 'executive detached' style, built as part of an Urban Priority Area initiative with some help from the Church Commissioners.

ways some clergy still have official rectories or vicarages. The names are familiar but the context has changed. There are now fewer benefices and fewer clergy, with a greater role played by local non-stipendiary and lay ministers without parsonages.

The life cycle of one parsonage shows these trends in practice. I was born in the Victorian vicarage at Holme, Huntingdonshire (now Cambridgeshire). The large, brick-built house of 1857 was nearing its century. It was typical of the heroic aspirations of the mid-nineteenth-century Church of England. Holme had been a chapelry in the parish of Glatton. In the early 1850s the great inland lake of Whittlesey Mere, on the edge of which Holme sat, was drained, turning the lake to farms. The main London–Edinburgh railway, opened in 1850, bisected this new, modern landscape. These transformations were recorded for the *Illustrated London News* by the curate of Glatton-with-Holme, Edward Bradley. Better known as Cuthbert Bede, he was finding time to write and illustrate his highly popular Verdant Green books, but found local duties hard. He lodged at the Woolpack Inn and wrote to

Holme Vicarage, Cambridgeshire, built in 1857 to serve a new fenland parish, and sold in 1970. It had been the hub of energetic and interventionist Victorian and Edwardian ministry.

a friend: 'At present my Rector is out and I have all the work with 3 full Duties on a Sunday together with Churchings and Baptisms & 8 miles of walking. And this for 75£ a year!'

To the re-energised Church of the 1850s this was an unsatisfactory situation, the more so given the new settlement out on the fen. Remedies were rapidly put in hand. In 1857 a new parish was created, where before there had been a ruinous chapel. A first step was to build a vicarage, with the glebe mortgaged to raise a loan of £825 from Queen Anne's Bounty. Then, between 1861 and 1862, the church was rebuilt, followed in 1868 by a new church school, both chiefly funded by the 'big house' family, the Wellses of Holmewood. Their burial place is at the church, and the local pub is the Admiral Wells. Church, school and parsonage were in place, but getting people to come to services and the children to come to school in all seasons, when some of them were 3 miles away across the fen and could get work there, required more effort. The school van was organised. Then, from 1897 to 1904 the vicar, George Broke, operated the Fen Ark. This floating church was drawn along the dykes by horse to places that could only be reached by water and brought Holy Communion, evensong and baptisms. The hub of all this activity was the vicarage. At the 1901 census the household consisted of Broke, his wife, their seven-year-old daughter and a visiting friend, together with four servants, all born elsewhere – a cook, a housemaid, a 'useful maid' and a parlour maid.

The Holme school van brought fenland children to the church school, which opened in 1868.

By the 1950s the picture was very different. My early childhood memories are of the spaciousness of the vicarage, its lawns, driveway and the big trees sheltering us from fenland winds. There was a coach-house, with fig tree growing against

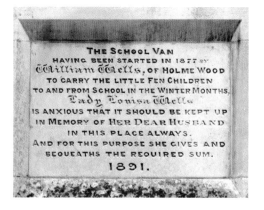

THE SCHOOL VAN
HAVING BEEN STARTED IN 1877 BY
William Wells, OF HOLME WOOD
TO CARRY THE LITTLE FEN CHILDREN
TO AND FROM SCHOOL IN THE WINTER MONTHS,
Lady Louisa Wells
IS ANXIOUS THAT IT SHOULD BE KEPT UP
IN MEMORY OF HER DEAR HUSBAND
IN THIS PLACE ALWAYS.
AND FOR THIS PURPOSE SHE GIVES AND
BEQUEATHS THE REQUIRED SUM.
1891.

the wall, but no coach. The rooms were high, with many books, but the comfort was limited with no mains water, and oil lamps and portable oil stoves requiring much tending. There was a radio, powered by big heavy batteries, which sprang slowly to life. There were certainly no servants and for my mother it was a life of some isolation and keeping up appearances. For my father, the vicar, soon to move on and without the private means of earlier times, there were worries about dilapidations.

Holme vicarage is now the Old Vicarage, much smarter and better appointed. It was sold in 1970, in favour of a modern vicarage built in the corner of the grounds. This served three benefices: Holme, Glatton and Conington. In 1997 there was another change when Holme with Conington was joined with Yaxley, where the incumbent now lives. He is assisted in serving Holme church by a retired non-stipendiary curate and an authorised lay minister. Holme's second vicarage has also been sold. Its life cycle as a parsonage, together with its predecessor of 1857, was short in historical perspective, yet epitomises major trends in parsonage history since 1850.

Holme's present-day village sign recalls the Fen Ark, a floating church towed along the dykes to outlying parts of the parish.

'Endless Appeal of Old Vicarages' – so ran a headline in *The Times* in 1997, and little seems to have diminished this, as former parsonages continue to change hands. Some new owners may embrace a sense of the role of the property, providing venues for fetes, events or meetings, perhaps financially supporting the church or serving as churchwarden. Others do not, firmly privatising the parsonage space. Some parsonages are no longer private houses, being subdivided for flats or converted as nursing homes. Yet others have been demolished and their sites developed. Some historic parsonages do retain their role, perhaps at the head of a

The fictional vicarage of 'St Saviour in the Marshes', an East London inner-city parsonage of the 2010s, as portrayed in the television series *Rev*.

team rectory. Elsewhere the 'four-bed, detached', outwardly little distinguishable from other contemporary homes, is the modern face of the parsonage. The portrayal in the television series *Rev* of life in a contemporary London inner-city vicarage has attracted interest and praise. Much persists from the long history of the parsonage, as the parson living amongst his flock strives to fulfil the established church's continuing obligation to offer ministry to all those living in his parish. The vicarage is at the centre of the work, a place of precariously balanced public and private, spiritual and practical cares and triumphs.

Ripe Old Rectory – a Sussex sign in 2014.

RIPE OLD RECTORY

FURTHER READING

(* indicates useful general surveys.)

*Barley, M. *Houses and History*. Faber and Faber, 1986 (especially chapters 7 and 12).

*Bax, B. A. *The English Parsonage*. John Murray, 1964.

Beresford, J. (ed.). *James Woodforde: The Diary of a Country Parson. 1758–1802*, Oxford University Press (World's Classics edition), 1935.

Bernard, G. W. *The Late Medieval Church*. Yale University Press, 2012.

Blythe, R. *Divine Landscapes*. Viking Penguin, 1986.

*Brittain-Catlin, T. *The English Parsonage in the Early Nineteenth Century*. Spire Books, 2008.

Church Commissioners. *Parsonages: A Design Guide*. Sixth edition, 1998.

Colman, S. 'Eye Vicarage: the Documentation of a Parsonage House' in *Proceedings of the Suffolk Institute of Archaeology and History*, XXXIV (1977), Part 1.

Coombs, H. and P. (editors). *John Skinner: Journal of a Somerset Rector, 1803–1834*. Oxford University Press, 1984.

Dymond, D. and Paine, C. *Five Centuries of an English Parish Church: The State of Melford church, Suffolk*. EAH Press, 2012.

Hartridge, R. A. R. *A History of Vicarages in the Middle Ages*. Cambridge University Press, 1930.

Hughes, A. (editor). *Sussex Clergy Inventories 1600–1750*. Sussex Record Society, volume 91, 2009.

*Jones, A. *A Thousand Years of the English Parish*. Windrush Press, 2000.

Knight, F. *The Nineteenth-Century Church and English Society*. Cambridge University Press, 1995.

Macfarlane, A. *The Family Life of Ralph Josselin: A Seventeenth Century Clergyman*. Cambridge University Press, 1970.

Enforced residence meant that the clergy pursued many parsonage pastimes. Canon Henry Ellacombe, vicar of Bitton, Gloucestershire from 1850, was a great plantsman and author, who saw in his gardening a link to his flock and 'a great lesson … that everything in nature is subject to the strictest law' that did not change.

McLeod, H. *Religion and Society in England, 1850–1914.* Macmillan Press 1996.

Obelkevich, J. *Religion and Rural Society: South Lindsey, 1825–1875.* Oxford University Press, 1976.

Orme, N. *Cornwall and the Cross: Christianity 500–1560.* Phillimore, 2007.

Owen, D. *Church and Society in Medieval Lincolnshire* (*History of Lincolnshire,* volume V). 1971.

*Platt, C. *Parish Churches of Medieval England.* Secker & Warburg, 1981.

*Pounds, N. J. G. *A History of the English Parish.* Cambridge University Press, 2000.

*Savidge, A. *The Parsonage in England: Its History and Architecture.* SPCK, 1964.

Smith, M. *Religion in Industrial Society: Oldham and Saddleworth, 1740–1865.* Oxford University Press, 1994.

Spufford, M. *Contrasting Communities: English Villagers in the Sixteenth and Seventeenth Centuries.* Cambridge University Press, 1974.

Stokes, F. G. (editor). *The Bletchley Diary of the Rev. William Cole.* Constable, 1931.

Stone, M. (editor). *The Diary of John Longe, Vicar of Coddenham, 1765–1834.* Suffolk Record Society, 2008.

Swanson, R. N. *Church and Society in Late Medieval England.* Blackwell, 1989.

Vaisey, D. (editor). *The Diary of Thomas Turner, 1754–1765.* Oxford University Press, 1984.

Woodforde, D. H. (editor). 'Nancy Woodforde. A Diary for the Year 1792' in *Woodforde Papers and Diaries.* Morrow & Co./Parson Woodforde Society, 1990.

TRACING THE HISTORY OF A PARSONAGE: A CHECKLIST OF SOURCES

Three principal **general listings** are:
- Taxatio Ecclesiastica (1291)
- Valor Ecclesiasticus (1535)
- Report of the Royal Commission on the Ecclesiastical Revenues of England and Wales (1835)

For more recent information see:
- Crockford's Clerical Directories (1858–)
- Church of England yearbooks

The main types of relevant record include:
- Bishops' registers, including ordination of vicarages
- Glebe terriers
- Probate inventories
- Benefice papers relating to parsonage houses and property, in parish papers and/or the personal or family papers of clergy
- Estate records of monastic and other appropriators, lay impropriators and patrons
- Drawings and prints of parsonages
- Diaries and letters
- Tithe apportionment records (following the legislation of 1836)
- Maps: county, estate, tithe and large-scale Ordnance Survey
- Census enumerators' returns (for clerical households, 1841–1911)
- Architects' plans, associated correspondence, mortgages (in the Church of England Record Centre or diocesan record offices, often part of county record offices)
- Printed contemporary illustrations and descriptions (e.g. *The Gentleman's Magazine; The Builder*; county and local antiquarian histories)
- Photographs and paintings
- Parsonage buildings themselves

If a place has been covered by the Victoria County History (VCH) series, the parsonage living and house will have been researched using a full range of sources. The local VCH will be a good place to start. All but the most recent published volumes are available at British History Online (www.british-history.ac.uk); draft entries are posted as work in progress at www.victoriacountyhistory. ac.uk/counties. Some original sources, e.g. the *Taxatio Ecclesiastica* of 1291, are available online, whilst collections of some, e.g. glebe terriers, have been published for some dioceses or counties. The websites of the National Archives (www.nationalarchives.gov.uk), the Church of England Record Centre (www. lambethpalacelibrary.org/content/cerc)and many local archives offer general and specific guidance on tracing parsonage and house history.

Other websites of possible interest include English Monastic Archives (www.ucl.ac.uk/history2/englishmonasticarchives), and the CCEd: Clergy of the Church of England database (http://theclergydatabase.org.uk) covering the period 1540–1835.

INDEX